Sustainability Delivered

Sustainability Delivered

Designing Socially and Environmentally Responsible Supply Chains

Madeleine Pullman and Margaret Sauter

Sustainability Delivered: Designing Socially and Environmentally Responsible Supply Chains
Copyright © Business Expert Press, LLC, 2012.

First published in 2012 by
Business Expert Press, LLC
222 East 46th Street, New York, NY 10017
www.businessexpertpress.com

ISBN-13: 978-1-60649-318-2 (paperback)

ISBN-13: 978-1-60649-319-9 (e-book)

DOI 10.4128/9781606493199

A publication in the Business Expert Press Supply
and Operations Management collection

Collection ISSN: 2156-8189 (print)
Collection ISSN: 2156-8200 (electronic)

Cover design by Jonathan Pennell
Interior design by Exeter Premedia Services Private Ltd.,
Chennai, India

First edition: 2012

10 9 8 7 6 5 4 3 2 1

Printed in the United States of America.

Abstract

Sustainability Delivered was written to help supply chain managers, entrepreneurs, executives, and stakeholders develop the awareness and skills needed to support sustainable supply chain management in their firms. The book introduces the many ways that social and environmental responsibility can be integrated into supply chain management, from sustainable product and process design to programs and techniques that support product end-of-life management. The book also explores how sustainable supply chain management can be a key contributor to a firm's competitive advantage. With case examples, workshops, and step-by-step instruction in how to create a sustainable supply chain, *Sustainability Delivered* is the most practical and usable book on the market for helping business leaders authentically pursue and deliver on sustainability ideals.

Keywords

Biomimicry, Certification programs, Cradle to Cradle (C2C), Design for Disassembly (DfD), Design for the Environment, Ecoefficiency, End-of-life management (EOL), Environmental management system (EMS), Environmentally responsible supply chain management, Extended product responsibility, Industrial ecology, ISO 14000, ISO 26000, Life Cycle Analysis, Life Cycle Assessment, The Natural Step, Process design, Product design, Product end-of-life management (EOL), Purchasing scorecards, Socially responsible supply chain management, Supplier assessment, Supplier scorecards, Sustainable supply chain management, Value stream mapping

Contents

Preface

More than ever before, companies are facing strong pressure to be more "sustainable." For some, this pressure is externally driven—by consumers, retail partners, activists, and regulators—while for others, the pressure is internal in nature, stemming from a profound interest in doing the right thing, a desire to limit business risk, and a keen awareness that sustainability can be an immense source of competitive advantage in today's business environment. No matter its origin, the need to reduce negative social and environmental impacts and increase social and environmental responsibility is very real for many companies today. Sustainable supply chain management is an excellent, authentic route to addressing this challenge.

This book was written to help managers, entrepreneurs, executives, and stakeholders develop the awareness and skills needed to support sustainable supply chain management in the firm. We begin by introducing the concept of sustainability, and detailing its application in the business world—specifically, issues surrounding social and environmental responsibility in industry, and the economic impact on companies that decide to take positive action. We dive further into these topics in chapter 2, discussing the relationship between business strategy and sustainability, and the impact that sustainable supply chain management can have on a firm's competitive potential.

In chapter 3, we start identifying the tools and techniques of sustainable supply chain management. We first address sustainable product and process design, offering instruction in value stream mapping, design for the environment, life cycle assessment, industrial ecology, cradle to cradle, and biomimicry, among other product and process development practices. In chapter 4, we discuss purchasing and logistics, which most influence the social and environmental impact of companies with long supply chains today. A "best practices" model for sustainable purchasing is articulated, detailing tools like codes of conduct, certification programs, and auditing and monitoring systems, and sustainable logistics strategies are introduced.

In chapter 5, we discuss product end-of-life management, and identify the different approaches that companies can take to "close the loop" in their supply chains and eliminate product waste. In our conclusion, we discuss what's next in the field of sustainable supply chain management, addressing trends and emerging practices.

In the interest of keeping this book accessible, concept illustrations are provided throughout, including case examples and mini-workshops.

The case examples illustrate sustainable supply chain management in action at some of the world's leading companies, both big and small. Mini-workshops provide step-by-step guidance to practitioners looking to apply ideas.

In closing, our goal in writing this book has been to give readers a practical, usable manual that demystifies sustainable supply chain management. We hope you enjoy the book, apply the ideas as they work for you, and excel at making sustainable supply chain management a core competency in your business, and a key contributor to your success.

Acknowledgments

We would like to thank the many people and organizations that contributed their support to this book. First, we would like to thank our research assistant, Whitney Dawson, for her help in identifying company examples and tirelessly researching topics and ideas, and Professor Desiree Pacheco for her insight into sustainability strategy. Second, we would like to thank Portland State University for funding graduate assistance programs, and the Loackers for generously funding the research grant program at Portland State's Center for Global Leadership in Sustainability. Third, we would like to thank the many local and national companies and organizations that provided interviews and examples for this book, including Sattie Clark of Eleek Inc., James Jedibudiah of Ovations Food Services, and Garett Brennan of Focus the Nation. And finally, we would like to thank our families for supporting us and allowing this book to happen: Tim Brill, and Matt and Sam Krapfl. Your patience and enthusiasm help us in everything we do.

CHAPTER 1

Sustainable Supply Chain Management

No matter your managerial role, the pressure to make your company more sustainable has likely risen in recent years. All industries, from food to electronics to pharmaceuticals, are being affected by increasing consumer and stakeholder interest in social and environmental issues. For many companies, particularly those in manufacturing and retail, these types of issues are most authentically addressed by evaluating and making changes to their supply chain. This book was written to help executives, managers, and other stakeholders work through this process.

To do this, this book discusses sustainability as it relates to three fundamental aspects of supply chain management: product and process design, purchasing and logistics, and **product end-of-life management**. Along the way, the connection between competitive business strategy and sustainable supply chain management is examined, and measurement and reporting issues are discussed. Best practices models are introduced where relevant, and every chapter features a Checklist for the Practicing Professional, giving managers quick action plans to help them start work. Numerous case examples are also provided herein, illustrating how companies across industries, of varying sizes, and at different points in their corporate life cycle have given life to their sustainability goals via sustainable supply chain management.

Before we launch into the "how to" of the sustainable supply chain, however, we need to cover the "what" and the "why." This chapter identifies the social and environmental issues that have, over time, surfaced as key concerns in supply chain management. We then discuss the economic argument for sustainability, and review the reasons why companies are transforming their supply chains to be more sustainable, despite the effort and perceived cost. We conclude this chapter with the data, and show that even with the global economic recession in full swing, an increasing number of companies are embracing sustainability, making it an ongoing factor in corporate competitiveness.

Sustainability: A Brief Overview

The word "sustainability" has many interpretations, but perhaps the most easily understood definition is that put forth in the *Brundtland Report*, a 1987 document produced by the United Nations' World Commission on Environment and Development, which addressed the impact of natural resources depletion on social and economic development worldwide. The report defined sustainable development as "an approach to progress which meets the needs of the present without compromising the ability of future generations to meet their own needs."[1] This definition has since been absorbed and transformed by the business community into the concept of the **triple bottom line**, in which people, planet, and profit—or social, environmental, and economic concerns—are of equal importance when measuring corporate performance, as all three must be in balance to ensure long term business stability and hence, prosperity.

Social, environmental, and economic issues are intrinsically interconnected in business, and today they are often discussed under the single rubric of "sustainability," as shown in Figure 1.1. Companies need to understand how sustainability issues intersect, as seemingly responsible choices in one realm—often demanded by consumers and stakeholders—may have untold consequences in another realm, thereby undermining a company's efforts to be truly sustainable. However, the operational focus of supply chain management also demands that managers have a deep comprehension of the primary issues in each of these realms individually, as a manager's failure to know what constitutes a responsible choice in any one area could significantly and negatively impact a company's image and performance overall. The people, planet, and profit issues that have emerged as key concerns in supply chain management are therefore discussed below.

Figure 1.1. Sustainability issues and the triple bottom line.

Social Issues (The "People")

The first sustainability concerns that surfaced in supply chain management focused on social justice issues, particularly wage violations and working conditions in apparel manufacturing in the late 1980s. Outcry over wages and working conditions soon spread to the use of child labor, the use of forced labor, prohibitions on the right to unionize, and violence and discrimination in the workplace.[2] Today, these problems still top the list of social concerns in supply chain management, particularly when the supply chain extends beyond the boundaries of the developed world. These concerns are summarized in Table 1.1.

Nike's debacle with soccer ball manufacturing illustrates this well. *Life* magazine ran a story in its June 1996 issue about child labor in Pakistan. The article showed a 12-year-old boy assembling pieces of a Nike soccer ball. Activists from North America quickly mobilized to protest in front of Nike outlets. A few months later, *48 Hours*, the CBS news program, ran a story that highlighted labor abuses at Nike's Vietnamese shoe manufacturing plant. The abuses included inhumane treatment

Table 1.1. Primary Social Concerns in Supply Chain Management

Issue	Concern	Common minimum standards
Wages	Wages are below a legally established minimum, nonpayment of wages, nonpayment of overtime	Unique to each country and work environment
Working time	Working hours so long that they do not give workers time to recuperate in a given day or week	60 hours per week with one day per week off
Health and safety	Work environments are unsafe: absent or blocked fire exits, lack of appropriate safety gear, etc.	Unique to each work environment
Child labor	Children work in factories and thus are diverted from other routes out of poverty, particularly education	No workers under the age of 16
Forced labor	Fees for job placement are paid by workers versus companies, or are excessive in nature; slave labor	Recruitment fees not in excess of 1 month's wages
Discrimination	Individuals are denied access to a job because of characteristics that do not prevent them from doing that job	Equal Opportunity clauses
Harassment and violence	Workers are intimidated in the work environment, as a means to dissuade them from improving conditions	No harassment and violence
Freedom to associate/right to collective bargaining	Workers are not allowed to form organizations that can leverage their power to improve conditions	Freedom to Associate and the Right to Collective Bargaining are acknowledged

Note: Although this list characterizes global social issues, they are also of concern domestically. U.S. labor laws and regulations are designed to address most of these issues; nonetheless, violations of U.S. law do occur.
Sources: STR Responsible Sourcing; United Nations Global Compact; International Labour Organization.

of workers by their supervisors, payment of wages below the legal minimum, and sexual abuse of several women workers. In both cases, Nike
employed subcontractors to manage the production of its products, as is
typical in the shoe, apparel, and sports gear industry.

While Nike had a **code of conduct** with its subcontractors—an
agreement detailing the company's position on wages and working
conditions—many felt this effort was insufficient to truly prevent abuse.
Worsening matters, Phil Knight, Nike's CEO, took a defensive position
when addressing the issue and ran into conflict with shareholders, consumers, and activist groups. Since then, Nike has taken a more proactive
stance on labor issues in its supply chain, and has made great headway in
both its social and environmental programs. However, the incident is still
remembered as an example of poor social integrity in supply chain management—and as such is a permanent stain on Nike's record.[3]

As noted, Nike claimed that a complexity in its supply chain—
subcontracting—prevented it from being aware of abuse at its suppliers'
facilities. For managers in many industries, this is and will continue to
be a frustrating trend. Globalization, specialization, and the subsequent
fragmentation of supply chains are leaving many companies in the dark
about what is going on in their **supplier tiers**, just as activists and the Internet are turning on the light. Figure 1.2 illustrates the concept of supplier
tiers, and demonstrates the complexity of managing such an operation.

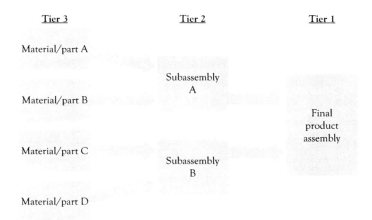

Figure 1.2. Supply chain tiers, often fragmented and global in scope.

One recent example of this is Apple Computer. Despite the company's reputation for product elegance, innovation, and progressive thinking, Apple's integrity was called into question by media reports of poor working and living conditions at one of its suppliers' facilities in China in 2006. In response to these reports, Apple audited the supplier to assess its adherence to the company's Supplier Code of Conduct, and subsequently audited all of its Mac and iPod final assembly manufacturers to assess their compliance as well.[4]

Minor violations of the Code were found and corrective actions were taken, but the company was again tarnished by reports of employee suicides at its Foxconn supplier in 2009 and 2010. The suicides, along with allegations of worker mistreatment, prompted Apple to investigate conditions at this first tier supplier, which was located in China. Apple found that Foxconn was improperly housing employees, forcing overtime, and underpaying wages. Audits of other suppliers revealed health risks from chemical exposure and the use of involuntary and underage labor—all of which required corrective action and in some cases, substantial employee compensation.[5]

Perhaps having learned a thing or two from Nike, Apple owned up to its labor issues in its annual *Supplier Responsibility Progress Report*, a document that lays bare the results of its ongoing supplier audit program. The report reveals the good and the bad in Apple's supply chain, and its content is a lesson in how difficult it can be for companies to ensure supply chain integrity when globalization and outsourcing are standard modes of operation. For instance, of the 127 facilities audited by Apple in 2010, 18 were found to have used "foreign contract workers who paid excessive recruitment fees to labor agencies"—a core violation of Apple's Code of Conduct that the company classified as involuntary labor.[6]

Cultural differences can influence the supply chain as well, also evidenced by this example. In some countries, recruitment fees are common. Thus, Apple has had to create rules on these fees that make clear what it considers to be the line between worker exploitation and worker assistance.[7] Levi Strauss has also noted that priorities deemed important by American consumers—such as the freedom to associate—are at times not recognized in the countries in which it operates: "In a number of countries, regardless of local labor law requirements, the right to freely associate is not widely observed." In these countries, Levi's has therefore had to work directly with companies to overcome "significant historical, social and legal obstacles" to workers' rights, at times leading to supplementary education, health, and safety programs.[8]

And it is here that crafting the socially responsible supply chain gets even more complicated. While some activities are universally acknowledged to be human rights violations—slave labor, sexual harassment, unsafe working conditions—vast discrepancies in the quality of life between consuming and producing countries often make it difficult for companies to determine what constitutes a "fair" wage, or a "reasonable" work week, or even the "right" age at which a child can work. Nike's 2007–2009 *Social Responsibility Report* articulates its operating context well:

> At the center of our footprint stand more than 800,000 workers in our contracted supply chain. Most of these workers are young women, many of whom are the first women in their family to work in the formal economy. This phenomenon has the potential to lead to significant social change in families and their communities, yet these workers are typically poorly educated, and living against a precarious backdrop of poverty and insecurity within emerging economies.[9]

With limited opportunities to work and poverty always on the horizon, the need to earn a living can often blur the line between a "just" and an "unjust" work environment, for both workers and employers. Nicholas Kristof, a columnist for *The New York Times*, recently reflected that sweatshops, for example, "are only a symptom of poverty, not a cause, and banning them closes off one route out of poverty." He continued, "In the hierarchy of jobs in poor countries, sweltering at a sewing machine isn't the bottom."[10] The United Nations' Global Compact, which helps promote sustainability in business, also recognizes the dilemma, this time with regard to child labor: "Dismissing children from the workplace may leave them vulnerable to more exploitative work elsewhere and [have] negative health and wellbeing implications due to increased poverty within the family (if, indeed they have [family])."[11]

Clearly, creating the socially responsible supply chain is a complex undertaking. Doing the "right" thing requires much more than a vague sense of corporate responsibility; it also requires more than generic codes of conduct enforced only at the first tier supplier level. The most socially responsible supply chains feature a knowledge of producer contexts at each activity tier—from raw materials sourcing to product recycling—around which meaningful labor standards are then established. These standards are then backed up by consistent auditing and corrective action. For companies with deep pockets, supplementary programs that address ongoing social, economic, and cultural issues can take the initiative even further.

Small companies may find this aspirational model intimidating, and wonder exactly how they fit in, given their own labor constraints. For managers of such companies, it's best to remember that some effort and interest in social responsibility is better than none at all. Additionally, numerous tools and organizations have come online in the last decade that are making the quest to be socially responsible much easier. These include **supplier scorecards** that can serve as a basis for research and standards-setting; publicized supplier lists put out by major companies that have undertaken robust social responsibility programs (e.g., Nike, Levi's), which can shorten the search for vetted suppliers in some industries; and well-regarded organizations that provide **third party certification** services for secondary and tertiary suppliers claiming to be responsible. Developing sustainability strategies in conjunction with existing supply chain partners can also spread the effort and costs of social responsibility, while benefiting all partners equally. All of these ideas—and other resources—are discussed in more detail in later chapters of this book.

Environmental Issues (The "Planet")

Although labor issues were the first sustainability concerns to strongly influence the field of supply chain management, the explosion of public interest in environmental issues in the 1960s and 1970s inevitably found focus in the way we source, manufacture, transport, consume, and dispose of raw materials and finished goods. This focus has only intensified as consumers have become more aware of how food, clothing, electronics, automobiles, and other tools of daily life are brought to their door.

Today, no industry is exempt from the pressure to "green" their supply chain, and environmental responsibility is almost synonymous with the term "sustainability."

Environmental concerns in supply chain management can be grouped into two basic categories—concerns about **inputs** and concerns about **outputs**—and the fundamental goal of green supply chain management is to reduce the negative impact of both of these on the environment, as shown in Table 1.2. With regard to inputs (e.g., water, oil, minerals), the focus is on minimizing their use and using renewable resources as inputs whenever possible. With regard to outputs (e.g., products, waste, pollution), the focus is on reducing, reusing, and recycling. The move to manage inputs and outputs more sustainably has broadened the scope of supply chain management to include activities like product design, and has created new work functions in supply chain management, like product end-of-life management.

Many companies have low-hanging fruit that, if picked, can enhance the environmental profile of their supply chain very quickly. Replacing incandescent light bulbs with compact fluorescent bulbs in factories, replacing worn out fleet vehicles with more fuel efficient trucks and vans, and reworking delivery schedules to reduce truck idling are well-known examples of easy supply chain improvements. These and other actions—particularly those related to energy and fuel efficiency—can also often reduce manufacturing and supply chain costs, improving a company's bottom line. These types of benefits make greening the supply chain very appealing.

Table 1.2. Primary Environmental Concerns in Supply Chain Management

Inputs		Outputs	
Common inputs	**Common concerns**	**Common outputs**	**Common concerns**
Water Oil Minerals Chemicals Lumber Plants Animals	Reducing use of initial inputs Using renewable resources as inputs	Consumer products Production waste Consumer waste Water pollution Air pollution Greenhouse gases	Reducing waste Recycling outputs for use as inputs elsewhere Appropriate toxic waste processing

Sources: The Story of Stuff.

For example, Kroger, one of the nation's largest grocery retailers, improved the efficiency of its fleet by 15.5% between 2008 and 2010 by increasing the fuel performance of its trucks, loading its trucks to capacity and reducing the transport of empty trailers. In light of these early successes, Kroger substantially upped its sustainability goals and now aims to increase its fleet efficiency by 40% by 2014, a notable target for a company that travels almost 300 million miles a year.[12] While Kroger has not released official information on the impact of these and other energy improvements to its bottom line, several reports have cited savings in the hundreds of millions of dollars.[13]

However, for every story about low-hanging fruit, there are many more examples that reveal just how complex environmentally responsible supply chain management can be. This is particularly true when a company's goal is to fundamentally rethink existing product lines, or to build new product lines that have sustainability features built in.

For example, Wal-Mart's first organic clothing products were stocked in an opportunistic way—if its first tier suppliers had good prices available on organic clothes, the products would find their way onto the racks at Wal-Mart and Sam's Club stores. Strong consumer interest indicated, however, that the company would benefit from building a consistent supply of organic textiles into its product array. This, in turn, required Wal-Mart to greatly reduce its product costs and ensure the legitimacy of its organic claims, given intense consumer scrutiny of nearly all of Wal-Mart's green initiatives.[14]

To reduce costs, Wal-Mart had to change the transactional nature of its buying process. Building long-term relationships with suppliers and giving them purchasing commitments encouraged farmers to go organic and increased the supply of organic cotton on the market, reducing prices. The company also had to revise its manufacturing process for organic clothing to eliminate extraneous product movement and handling, further reducing costs. Lastly, Wal-Mart adopted the Global Organic Textiles Standard for organic cotton, which is a highly regarded third party certification standard.[15] All told, Wal-Mart's organic textiles program took several years to develop and required numerous changes to its well-honed supply chain processes.

Poor development of initial supply chain systems can also challenge green management. **Take-back** programs, in which manufacturers accept returns of used products for recycling or reuse, can benefit companies by reducing their need to buy new inputs, or by giving them a new revenue stream from the sale of waste products to recyclers. However, take-back initiatives require well-developed reverse logistics programs, and if the waste is to be reused by the manufacturer, they also require well-developed forecasting and inventory management systems so that manufacturers do not run out of their supply of "new" manufacturing parts. Incorporating take-back goals into the product design process is therefore essential if such initiatives are to be successful and worthwhile. As Steve Jobs noted:

> Producers must…take responsibility for the design and material choices that create the product in the first place. It is these choices that fundamentally determine the weight and recycling value of the material waste at the end of a product's life…Our designs use aircraft-grade aluminum, stainless steel and high-grade plastics that are in high demand from recyclers, who recover and resell these raw materials for use in other types of products.[16]

Finally, external factors can complicate a company's quest to go green, and must therefore be considered when crafting a sustainability plan. For example, Ovations Food Services, a food service vendor that services over 100 locations including major sports arenas, convention centers, gaming facilities, and fairgrounds nationwide, wanted to pursue a zero waste program in which all food waste and food production by-products in its facilities would be diverted to either composting or biodiesel production. This vision, illustrated in Figure 1.3, reflects the essence of the **closed loop** concept, in which the outputs of one process are used as the inputs for another process. However, this vision was complicated by the almost total lack of industrial composting and biodiesel production facilities nationwide. One national survey of haulers in the locations where Ovations worked revealed that some regions didn't even have recycling programs, never mind the infrastructure to support food waste or grease processing. The company therefore has had to phase in its ambitious zero waste program, starting in locations where external support services exist.[17]

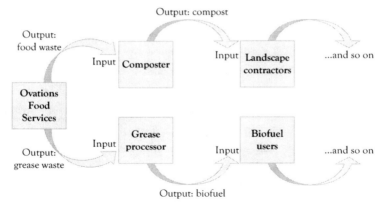

Figure 1.3. Example of a closed loop system (Ovations Food Services).

As should be evident, green supply chain management can be both easy and frustratingly hard. The basic concepts associated with environmental responsibility are not difficult to understand—responsible sourcing; reducing, reusing, and recycling; using outputs as inputs; etc.—but actual implementation of these ideas often goes against ingrained business thinking and practices. For projects that require extensive creativity, risk, discipline, or technical know-how, or in which a strong dependence on external partners exists, leadership buy in is essential, and a firm business case must also typically be made. Nearly every chapter in this book is geared to build up the tangible skills of the green manager—from **life cycle analysis** to the use of metrics—but the business case will be unique from industry to industry, and from company to company. That being said, the next section lays out the basic economic argument for sustainable supply chain management, which managers will need to assess for applicability to their own situation.

Economic Issues (The "Profit")

Just as the quality revolution of the 1980s pushed a seemingly counterintuitive agenda, in which increased investment in certain aspects of management and production—like goal setting, training, and continuous improvement—could improve the bottom line of many companies, sustainability advocates often promote the idea that the movement's holistic approach to business can reap benefits beyond those directly projected on paper. The legitimacy of this idea has surely been questioned by countless managers in countless companies throughout the world. Academia, too, has had its suspicions, and hundreds of business studies have tested the purported financial benefits of sustainability, also termed "corporate social performance" (CSP) by some.

The results of these studies have been mixed. In search of a definitive answer, researchers from several top tier schools in 2007 conducted a meta-analysis of 167 studies that assessed the relationship between corporate social and corporate financial performance (CFP). They found that a "mildly positive relationship" appears to exist between CSP and CFP, and that although "companies do not seem to be richly rewarded for engaging in CSP," they are "not overly [financially] penalized for CSP investments," either.[18] The research also indicated that there was a high level of variability between financial performance and different CSP activities (e.g., contributions to charity, creating corporate policies), and a general lack of clarity regarding causality in the data. For example, it cannot be determined if companies get a strong financial boost from donating to charitable causes, or if they are donating to charitable causes because they have a strong bottom line to begin with, and thus the financial ability to do so.

The lack of ability to conclusively determine the financial impact of CSP initiatives encouraged the authors of this particular study to state that "the continuing quest to substantiate or repudiate a link between CSP and CFP may be of little value."[19] After conducting a sizeable literature review in service of this question, we've decided that we agree. Moreover, after interviewing numerous managers in the field who are tackling sustainability from different angles, it seems almost self-evident that the answer to whether or not sustainability can "pay" depends heavily on a company's industry and operating context, size and scale, overall financial health, development of fundamental business systems, the extent and nature of the initiative under consideration, and the skills of those leading the effort, among other factors.

That being said, opinions on sustainability's benefits do seem to have coalesced around a certain set of observations, as summarized in Table 1.3. Stated benefits include improved marketability; enhanced worker morale and thus, productivity; reduced risk and risk-related

Table 1.3. Common Stated Benefits of Sustainability Initiatives

Benefit	Rationale
Enhanced marketability	Brand value increases if consumers feel a company values more than just profits; brand reputation can also be more easily maintained if the risk of doing the wrong thing is reduced and if consumers have loyalty.
Reduced risk	More conscientious management of a company's supply chain improves its ability to prevent social and environmental disasters, which helps reduce mitigation costs and brand rebuilding costs.
Reduced costs	Fuel and energy efficiency, in addition to lean manufacturing methods, can reduce waste in operations and the supply chain, thereby reducing production costs and improving margins.
Higher prices	Green consumers are interested in sustainable products and are willing to pay a premium for these projects. Higher consumer prices can result in higher margins, if costs are contained.
Improved employee morale	Employees feel good working for a company that is striving to do the right thing, and if they are engaged in company improvement efforts. They therefore become more productive and improve the bottom line.
Regulatory opportunities	Being first in line has given some companies the opportunity to help create new regulations related to sustainability; retrofitting operations to match new regulatory frameworks is also costly.
Supply chain distinction	Sustainability's focus on relationships and collaboration build trust in the supply chain. This can make suppliers wary of selling to others, thereby creating unique and hard-to-replicate supply chains.
Shared efforts/costs	Complicated sustainability efforts often necessitate collaboration in the supply chain. This spreads the creative effort and costs of sustainability to partners, who then each partake in the rewards.

Sources: Author notes; Accenture/United Nations Global Compact 2010 CEO Survey.

costs; and unique opportunities to shape future regulatory frameworks. With regard to supply chain management, additional benefits include the opportunity to develop hard-to-replicate supply chains, the chance to share the effort and cost of sustainability initiatives with partners in a supply chain, and the often significant opportunity to reduce operating costs via aforementioned energy, fuel, and manufacturing efficiencies, sometimes called **ecoefficiencies**.

The opportunity to develop a unique and differentiated supply chain is particularly robust in the food industry. As an example, Bon Appétit Management Company, a division of the Compass Group, has sourced sustainable, local foods for the 400 cafes it manages across the United States since 1999. Specific purchasing programs exist for nearly all of the food served by Bon Appétit, including meat, seafood, dairy, and eggs. Chefs are expected to look locally for their ingredients, to build long-term relationships with suppliers, and to support new, local producers that are attempting to bring their products to market.

The deep, collaborative relationships that Bon Appétit has with its suppliers gives the company a high level of security regarding ingredient quality and supply—particularly important when external factors, like weather, can compromise harvest and delivery without much warning. As an early adopter of sustainability principles in the food service industry, Bon Appétit was also able to gain significant market share by having a fully operational and marketable program just as institutional clients were becoming interested in sustainable food issues. Thus, Bon Appétit today has a long roster of high-value clients, including eBay, adidas, Yahoo!, the Target Corporation, the Art Institute of Chicago, and private colleges and universities nationwide.[20]

As noted, the opportunity to spread the effort and costs of sustainability to other suppliers in a value chain—who then also share in the rewards of higher market share and higher margins—is an additional benefit of sustainable supply chain management. Indeed, a 2010 CEO survey conducted by Accenture and the United Nations Global Compact indicated that 78% of CEOs believe "companies should engage in industry collaborations and multi-stakeholder partnerships to address development goals."[21] There are many examples of this today, particularly in industries that require substantial creativity and innovation to achieve sustainability goals, or in which economies of scale have not yet been realized for certain materials and products.

For example, Patagonia was the first company of its size to use fleece made from recycled soda bottles in its products, and organic cotton. Both materials require more labor during production than is standard, in addition to enhanced production knowledge and skills. The switch to organic cotton in particular was costly and difficult, but by sharing its knowledge and practices with others in the industry—including Marks & Spencer,

Timberland, Nike, Gap, and Wal-Mart—Patagonia was able to increase raw material demand and decrease costs.[22] Consumer knowledge about the company's efforts also helped drive sales, although this outcome was never a stated goal; Patagonia's cotton sales rose 25%.[23]

As a final point in the economic argument for sustainability, companies that are thinking of moving their supply chains in a more sustainable direction should consider this basic fact: after many years and many doubters, sustainability doesn't seem to be going away. In fact, nearly every major executive survey in recent years has noted an increase in the number of companies considering or pursuing a sustainability agenda. This is true even in surveys conducted after the onset of the recession.

The 2010 Accenture survey, which was the largest CEO study conducted to date on the topic of sustainability, indicated that 93% of CEOs see sustainability as important to their company's future success, and 88% believe they should be integrating sustainability into their supply chain. The study cited brand strength, consumer trust, and company reputation as the strongest motivators in the drive to become sustainable, with 72% of CEOs listing these among their top three reasons for taking action on sustainability. The potential for revenue growth and cost cutting were a distant second, with 44% of CEOs listing these concerns among their top three sustainability factors. Personal motivation and consumer demand were cited as factors by 42% and 39% of CEOs, respectively; employee engagement and recruitment garnered 31% of CEO votes; and regulatory pressure and pressure from investors and stakeholders were at the bottom, with 24% and 12% of CEOs considering these among their most pressing concerns.[24]

A 2010 Sustainability & Innovation survey of global corporate leaders conducted by The Boston Consulting Group and *MIT Sloan Management Review* confirmed Accenture's general findings. This survey was administered to company leaders who are not necessarily members of the United Nations Global Compact, which is dedicated to sustainability, and thus is perhaps more reflective of the opinions of the overall business community than the Accenture study. Nevertheless, it found that 52% of survey participants feel sustainability has a "permanent" place on management's agenda, and that 57% feel sustainability is necessary to be competitive today. Branding issues again took the lead in reasons to pursue sustainability.[25]

The Accenture survey also concurred with the BCG/*MIT* survey on one final, interesting point. Both surveys found the need to make the business case for sustainability was no longer business leaders' most pressing sustainability concern. The BCG/*MIT* survey quotes Peter White, the director of global sustainability at Proctor & Gamble, as saying, "from our point of view, it's a done deal—it's proven, let's get on with it."[26] The Accenture survey notes that in 2007, CEOs indicated a strong need for support in making the business case for sustainability. Accenture reports that today, "CEOs believe that execution is the real challenge." This sentiment echoes the gap found by Accenture between sustainability intention and reality: while 88% of CEO respondents felt they should be integrating sustainability into their supply chain, only 54% of CEOs felt this had actually been accomplished.[27]

We don't doubt that most of our readers are still interested in the business case for sustainability in their companies, no matter what global leaders have to say. However, in many cases, the precise benefits and costs of a more sustainable approach to doing business may be impossible to quantify until work is underway, just as the financial impact of a quality improvement initiative may be hard to predict before work begins. In lieu of exact numbers, a more conceptual understanding of the merits and drawbacks of sustainability for your firm may be worth developing. Chapter 2 provides instruction into how to develop this understanding, focusing on the operating conditions that encourage sustainability success, the generic business strategies that best support sustainability initiatives, and the specific benefits of sustainable supply chain management for competitive advantage.

Conclusion

This chapter introduced the concept of sustainable supply chain management. A straightforward definition of sustainability was presented, and the main social and environmental concerns that have emerged in supply chain management over the past three decades were explored. We learned that a continuum of goals and supporting activities exist in sustainable supply chain management, from basic efforts that aim to reduce operating costs, like ecoefficiencies, to more complex initiatives that can require the reconstruction of an entire supply chain, like a new, sustainable product line. We concluded this chapter with an assessment of the business case for sustainability. A self-evident point emerged: that the case for sustainability varies greatly between different industries, companies, and the project or concept at hand. We also learned that many business leaders today are no longer interested in debating the case for sustainability. Rather, they are looking to make sustainability a fundamental part of their strategy, and to execute on high value ideas. The remainder of this book addresses these learning needs directly.

Checklist for the Practicing Professional

Checklists for the Practicing Professional are featured in every chapter of this book, to help managers start incorporating sustainability concepts into their supply chain(s). As this chapter was introductory in nature, general questions are provided below. These questions are explored in more detail in later chapters:

- What is the general layout of your company's current supply chain(s)?
- How many tiers are in your company's supply chain(s)?
- What social concerns might exist within those tiers?
- What environmental issues might exist within or between the tiers?
- Are there complexities in your supply chain that might complicate sustainability?
- Are there opportunities in your supply chain that might ease its introduction?

Recommended Readings and Videos

Leonard, Anne. *The Story of Stuff* (www.storyofstuff.com). This is an excellent animated video that explains the basic components of a supply chain, from raw materials sourcing to consumer waste. It also presents sustainability concerns in supply chain management in an easy to understand manner.

Accenture/United Nations Global Compact (2010). *A New Era of Sustainability.* This report presents the results of a 2010 survey of 766 CEOs on sustainability issues in business. The report discusses motivating factors and key concerns. Numerous industries and companies are represented.

The Boston Consulting Group/*MIT Sloan Management Review* (2011). *Sustainability: the 'Embracers' Seize Advantage.* This report evaluates the sustainability adoption curve in business, particularly in light of the recession. It groups companies into two primary categories: "cautious adopters" and "embracers." The study's conclusions are based on a 2010 survey of global business leaders.

CHAPTER 2

Planning for Sustainability in the Supply Chain

Companies can do many things to be more sustainable. However, as noted in chapter 1, not all sustainability initiatives are the same. Different actions have different risk and return profiles, from low-risk, high-return ecoefficiencies, to bolder moves like reworking a product line to be more green, or launching a new company that has social and environmental improvement goals at its core. Thus, while many companies today see little need to justify ecoefficiencies, which are often easy to implement and widely acknowledged to benefit the bottom line, most companies will want to analyze the benefits and drawbacks of major sustainability initiatives before taking them on.

This chapter aims to assist with this analysis. We first discuss the business conditions that we believe are needed for authentic sustainability initiatives to be successful. We then examine the relationship between sustainability and business strategy, offering insight into how some well-known strategies support social and environmental goals, while others are less synergistic. We discuss how sustainable supply chain management can be a source of competitive advantage for a company. We conclude with a strategic planning workshop, designed to clarify readers' depth of interest in sustainability and think through implementation, including supply chain planning. Altogether, the contents of this chapter should help readers assess if their company is ready and willing to make a substantial and authentic move toward social and environmental responsibility, which is what the remainder of this book offers practical instruction in doing.

Note that we anticipate that different readers are going to be at different points in their business development processes—some belonging to well-established companies that need or want to launch new products, or that want to change direction completely; others having great ideas for a new sustainable business. Therefore, we have done our best to design the content of this chapter for both audiences. While established businesses may find some of the material or language to be rudimentary, we encourage all companies contemplating a significantly new course of action to at least skim this chapter before starting work, as it may surface issues and ideas that are important to consider before a more sustainable approach to business is pursued.

Conditions for Success

The incredible success of so many mission-driven companies over the last few decades has disproven the idea that social and environmental goals invariably sink a company's bottom line. At the same time, sustainable businesses are still businesses, and as such they need to regularly turn a profit if they are to stay in business, and thus continue to work toward their more substantive goals. To help companies that are considering sustainability as a new direction, and fledgling companies that are surveying the landscape, four "success factors" are discussed below—common characteristics that we have seen among companies that have had both mission and business success. Readers are encouraged to consider to what extent these factors exist in their situation, and what this means for their business plans.

Passion

Passion is a fundamental prerequisite of sustainable business success. Passion for an idea, purpose or goal can help a company create a compelling story for its products, and can help a company take the leap when the unique risks associated with social or environmental responsibility surface (e.g., higher raw material or labor costs, reliance on an untested business model, etc.). For a startup, passion is particularly important, helping founders soldier on when resources are tight, when failure feels like it is only a few days away, and when substantial creativity is needed to see an idea come to fruition.

An example of the importance of passion is TOMS, a company founded in 2006 on the premise of "one for one." The company's first product was TOMS Shoes, which gives away one pair of new shoes to a child in need for every pair of shoes sold. Recently, the company launched TOMS Eyewear, which similarly supports those in need with glasses and vision treatment for each pair of eyewear sold. The depth of social benefit TOMS was aiming to create when it was founded went far beyond standard **corporate philanthropy**. In turn, that meant the company had extremely limited resources in its early days; the enthusiasm of early "employees" helped TOMS succeed, despite the absence of steady paychecks and other resources.

> Because the concept of giving a product away to match a product sold was unique, we had no proven model to convince others to back us. The truth is, we didn't even know if it would work; therefore, it was difficult for us to raise money the way someone starting a traditional business does.[1]

Passion carried TOMS before its message took root with consumers. However, this example also illustrates the impact of passion on a business beyond its power to give employees energy, endurance, and creativity. The depth of a company or entrepreneur's passion can also profoundly affect its business model and practices. A schematic of sustainability-focused business practices is presented in Table 2.1, showing the variety of approaches that exist today to support social and environmental initiatives, including **social enterprise**, **corporate social responsibility**, and corporate philanthropy.

When deciding on a business approach, companies need to ask themselves: Is the primary purpose of my business to achieve a greater good, or is the primary purpose of my business to be in business, with social and environmental priorities pursued as best they can be? Any answer to this question is legitimate and fair, and in reality, even the most passionate and mission-driven companies will vacillate in their answer to this question from time to time. Nonetheless, knowing where your organization stands on its fundamental purpose will help it define a business model and strategy that match its level of passion, a key need for sustainable business success.

Table 2.1. Approaches to Supporting Social and Environmental Goals

	Social enterprise	Corporate social responsibility	Corporate philanthropy
Purpose	Explicit purpose is to create social or environmental benefit through operations	Adheres to socially and environmentally responsible principles during operations	Profits created through normal operations are directed to issues and causes of special interest
Legal structure	Benefit corporations, nonprofits, standard*	Benefit corporations, standard*	Standard*, often have a separate foundation to distribute funds or an associated nonprofit to conduct mission-driven activities
Stakeholders	Those impacted by operations, and owners, partners, members, and shareholders	Owners, partners, members, shareholders, and those impacted by operations	Owners, partners, members, shareholders
Operations	Operations designed to create social or environmental benefits	Operations respect and address social and environmental issues	Standard; may be unaffected by social or environmental goals
Supply chain	Often localized	Local or global	Local or global
Example	TOMS Shoes	Nike	Boeing

*"Standard" means any of the common business entities—such as an LLC, S Corporation, C Corporation, etc.

Leadership

Passion alone will rarely result in business success; good leaders are also needed to drive stakeholders toward a common vision. This is particularly true for sustainably minded companies, which are often pursuing goals that challenge common assumptions about how business gets done, or bringing products to market that are unique in some way. These activities carry risk, and therefore require a careful balance of visionary and pragmatic leadership. In this, new and existing companies tend to have different needs.

New companies often have the passion built right in; it comes hand in hand with the vision and drive that were required to start the whole venture in the first place. However, the enthusiasm of the entrepreneur may need to be tempered by real-world pragmatism—the challenge being to channel the entrepreneur's vision and energy into a viable business construct. If an experienced and competent business leader needs to be brought in to do this task, this should be done selectively. Crafting a trusting, positive, collaborative partnership at the leadership level is critical to a new venture's success.

In contrast, existing businesses come equipped with leaders that (hopefully) already know how to run a company. The challenge for these organizations is to get out of the rut of solely profit-driven thinking and into a mindset in which risks and rewards are newly embraced. This, in turn, means that leaders of existing businesses may have to convince legacy staff and stakeholders (investors, buyers, suppliers, etc.) that a company's new direction is worthwhile—either because it is a proactive move toward something beneficial (socially, environmentally, or financially), or because it is the best defense against an existing or upcoming threat. Thus, political and persuasive skill is a leadership need, as is the ability to translate sustainability goals and achievements into the value system and "language" already used by stakeholders.

Note as well that there may be a point when leaders of existing companies simply need to draw a line in the sand, eliminating old stakeholders who can't get on board, if possible, and recruiting new stakeholders who will. This is a perfectly reasonable course for companies pursuing a major transition, if efforts to get obstructionist or uninformed stakeholders on board have genuinely failed.

No matter a company's stage of development, leaders of sustainable businesses must have a deep understanding of the social and environmental contexts of the businesses they are running. In short, if a company's leaders do not understand the social or environmental implications of the strategies their company is adopting, and the tactics that will be executed in support of those strategies, it is going to be very difficult for that company to make balanced choices that ultimately serve a sustainability-oriented mission. Likewise, if your leader doesn't really share divisional or employee initiatives to be more sustainable, it is going to be difficult to educate that leader about the social and environmental side of the business, and to get substantial, high-level support for unproven, risky, or innovative ideas of any kind. If this is your situation, you may want to bring your great ideas to a different, like-minded employer.

Agility

Companies that want to be sustainable must also be innovative and flexible—particularly those that make things or that have a sizeable supply chain. This is because sustainable business standards and practices are still evolving, generally and within individual industries. Additionally, the conceptual frameworks, work processes, materials, and metrics used by a company to pursue its social and environmental goals are usually somewhat customized, responding to the specific priorities the business is attempting to address, and the conditions in which it is operating. Therefore, companies that are authentically working toward sustainability will want to continuously adjust and improve their approach and methods, aiming to do better. In short, most successful sustainable businesses are also learning organizations—that is, they have organizational cultures and work processes that encourage continuous improvement.

Ability to Make Good Compromises

It may not be popular, but it is certainly disingenuous to suggest that sustainably minded companies never think about their margins or the bottom line. While profits may not be the primary focus of a mission-driven company, a consistent lack of profits will prevent a business from continuing, and thus achieving the social or environmental good it set out to accomplish in the first place. This, in turn, means that compromise is often necessary, the goal being to make compromises that are thoughtful and informed.

For example, Patagonia is revered in the sustainable apparel industry for its relentless focus on quality and environmental responsibility, and its disregard for profit maximization. As Patagonia's founder, Yvon Chouinard, noted, Patagonia is "not constrained by the bottom line at all. We're constrained by the fact that some technologies don't exist yet."[2] At the same time, Patagonia has had to make choices that at least respect its bottom line—for instance, the company's decision to not manufacture all of its clothing in the United States.

This is as much a function of industry and quality constraints as it is of cost constraints. The company notes that "at one point nearly half our products were made in the U.S., but that percentage has steadily declined as textile and sewing operations have moved offshore. Now only the simplest styles can be sewn in the U.S. to high quality standards at a commercially viable cost."[3] However, both quality and cost influence a company's bottom line—quality being an attribute for which Patagonia's customers will pay a price premium, which boosts revenues; and cost management helping the company achieve reasonable margins. Chouinard himself notes the problem: "I could make everything domestically, but I would be out of business so fast I would become a martyr."[4]

Thus, the question for the sustainably minded business is not whether or not to compromise, it's usually when to compromise, and how to compromise well. Patagonia has compromised by taking much of its manufacturing overseas, versus sacrificing quality or demolishing its margins. However, it has also been mindful as it has gone overseas. The company has not pursued lowest-cost manufacturing. Rather, it has aimed to find factories that reflect its values, while meeting its quality and cost constraints; the company has a code of conduct, conducts supplier audits, and is extremely transparent about the successes and failures of its supply chain from the social and environmental perspective. The company has also assessed the impact of its longer transportation network on its carbon output and energy use, and determined it to be negligible due to the expanded use of more efficient transportation methods: boats, rail, etc.[5]

In conclusion, as long as businesses are faced with constraints, which all businesses are, choices will need to be made. And, as long as choices need to be made, compromise is likely. This in turn reinforces the need for the aforementioned success factors: passion, leadership, and agility. All of these attributes are necessary for companies to set high goals that extend far beyond profit, while making creative, mindful compromises that don't fundamentally work against their stated vision, mission, or values.

Sustainability and Strategy

Sustainability can be intimidating. Many businesses want to do the right thing, but defining the "right thing" can be hard, and following through can be harder still. In particular, developing the knowledge, frameworks, processes, materials, and metrics needed to substantially improve social and environmental impacts can seem like a huge and mysterious undertaking. While this book takes the general view that the best way to start being more sustainable is to simply dive in and learn by doing, we also think that critical reflection on your business's overarching strategy is worthwhile, as business strategy directly influences the goals, parameters, design, functioning, and resourcing of operational activities, like supply chain management. This section therefore examines the intersection of sustainability and business strategy.

"Strategy" has many definitions; most commonly, it is defined as a "theory of how to compete."[6] As such, strategy is thought to be a critical factor in firm performance and profitability. Good strategy should help a company consistently compete well and achieve sustained profitability; in other words, it should help a company achieve a **competitive advantage** over others in the market. Bad strategy will hinder a company as it tries to compete.

Sustainably minded companies may wonder if strategy is relevant to them. If the core purpose of strategy is to help a firm gain a competitive advantage in the market and outcompete others economically, does it conceptually align with the philosophy and values of sustainability? Many sustainably minded firms collaborate as much as they compete; want a win/win as much as an outright advantage; and want their business to generate more than just profits as an outcome. So, is strategy relevant for a sustainably focused firm? Is competitive advantage an ethically compatible goal?

We feel the answer to both of these questions is a clear "yes," however, not because competitive advantage and sustained profitability are meaningful ends in their own right, as business theory has traditionally suggested. Rather, we think these are valid achievements because they are an essential means to something better—necessary preconditions for businesses to do lasting social and environmental good. With effective strategy and sustained profits, mindful companies can consistently direct resources toward efforts that further social and economic equity, and increase industry reliance on renewable resources. These outcomes are not just innately better than profit, in our opinion, but they are also essential for industry to continue. This, in turn, suggests that the ultimate purpose of business is not to make money, as many have suggested. Rather, the purpose of a business is to create an enduring value cycle in which all parties benefit, and are able to participate in the cycle once again.

Which brings us back to the question of strategy. If strategy is an essential ingredient in business success, what strategies best align with and support sustainability ideals?

Strategies for Sustainability

Many business strategies exist, but two are particularly enduring and dominate business theory: **cost leadership** and **differentiation**, first defined by Michael Porter in his seminal book, *Competitive Strategy*. While many companies employ other strategies, these archetypes are useful in a discussion about sustainable business strategy because they reflect the two main concerns that all businesses have: keeping costs down, and keeping prices up.

In cost leadership, a company drives down costs in order to outperform competitors. Firms that adhere to this strategy are typically selling in mature markets in which products have become so uniform, or so commoditized, that the only way they can compete is on the basis of price. Because prices are low, a company must find cost advantages wherever it can if its margins are to be maintained—for example, producing in high volume, which enables economies of scale, or making technological investments that reduce the need for labor. If the risks of fixed costs are too high, as they might be in an uncertain or declining economy, a cost leader might choose to forgo fixed investments and instead make all of its costs variable—that is, to outsource. For companies that outsource, supply chain management is obviously an opportunity for competitive advantage. The goal is to have a supply chain that is lean, highly utilized, and high-performing on a cost per unit basis. Therefore, suppliers are selected on the basis of cost, and physical efficiency and throughput are essential performance factors.[7]

With differentiation, a company focuses on driving up the perceived value of its products, and thus its prices, in order to compete. Value can be increased by a company's reputation, by unique services that come with a product (e.g., customer support), or by a product's features, such as sustainability attributes that distinguish a product from its non sustainable counterparts. Because prices for differentiated products are higher than those for commodity products, margins for differentiated products can be larger. However, operating costs are also often much higher, due to smaller scale production, higher labor costs, and higher material costs. If a company is not vertically integrated, it will also need to invest in the development of a supply chain that is responsive, flexible, and capable of handling product variety and demand uncertainty—key characteristics of differentiated product lines.[8] All of these factors can substantially diminish margins, thus costs still need to be managed in a differentiated strategy. However, they are not the sole driver of strategy, as they are in a cost leadership situation.

An example of differentiation can be seen at Eleek, a company that designs and manufactures architectural fixtures in Portland, Oregon. The company's clients include architects, who order custom lighting, hardware, metal sinks, and metal tile countertops, and private clients, who buy fixtures from the company's small product line, advertised online and in select building supply stores nationwide. Eleek has focused on crafting custom, high-quality products since its founding in 2000, and, as co-founder Sattie Clark relays, "We were interested in sustainability from the get-go, particularly the use of recycled materials in our products." Thus, socially and environmentally responsible business practices are built into the company's business model, and are a key source of differentiation in the market. All of the company's castings are made of recycled metal (the exception being pewter, which cannot contain post-consumer recycled content), and all of its manufacturing is done locally, using highly skilled employees who receive living wages and excellent benefits.[9]

While Eleek's labor costs are higher than those of similar companies that manufacture overseas, the company's focus on sustainability actually helps with cost management. Keeping production local means the company can own the quality control process, which greatly reduces rework, waste, and associated costs, and helps the company maintain its strong reputation among clients. In this, Eleek also made a unique and conscious choice about how to grow. Clark notes,

> You have to make a choice in business: does it scale up? If so, how does it scale up? We could have easily had our products made in China. But that relates back to your embedded values. We knew going into this business that the U.S. had huge problems because we don't make anything here anymore. So when we thought about scaling up by making cheap parts overseas—well, it wasn't going to happen. We support our economy, our economy gets stronger, and the stronger the economy is the stronger our business can be.[10]

Clearly, differentiation is an important strategy for sustainable business development. As consumers will pay more for "value," which in the context of a sustainable business is the opportunity to enable a greater good by buying that particular product over spending money on something else, companies will have more financial room to innovate, take risks, and develop business models, products, processes, and supply chains that support that perception of value. Examples of value-driven activities and investments include:

- Investments in innovation (e.g., investing in sustainable product and process design activities, like life cycle assessment or biomimicry; investing in the innovation and development of more sustainable materials, like fully compostable plastics, etc.);
- Investments in higher material or labor costs (e.g., sourcing recycled materials, building or renting the dedicated equipment needed to work with organic materials, buying or renting hybrid vehicles, using biofuels, paying workers a living wage, offering great benefits, etc.);

- Investments in control mechanisms (e.g., supplier audits, certification fees); and
- Taking on costs that were formerly externalized (e.g., creating and running product take-back programs, to ensure products are appropriately processed after the end of their useful life).

Note that the utility of a differentiation strategy for launching a sustainable business doesn't mean a cost leadership strategy precludes investment in sustainability. Ecoefficiencies are a prime example of straightforward sustainability investments that have clear environmental and economic benefits and virtually no risk—perfect for those that need or want to pursue a cost leadership strategy, but that also want to work toward something more than just profit. Likewise, many cost leaders express support for social and environmental causes through corporate philanthropy and employee volunteer programs, the costs of which are ideally offset by a slight bump in the market value of the company's products, or a decrease in costs due to increased employee morale and productivity. If obtained, these offsets should help pay for the initiatives, while the company does more social or environmental good than it would otherwise.

However, differentiation clearly gives a company a sustainability advantage: more room to innovate, take risks, and make sustainability investments, as generically illustrated in Figure 2.1. In this, cost leaders interested in pursuing sustainability may want to consider its utility in helping them escape commoditized markets. An example of a company doing this is Columbia Forest Products (CFP), the largest manufacturer of hardwood plywood and veneer products in North America.

As the plywood industry is mature, and therefore affected by high rivalry, fierce competition, and declining margins, CFP thought it might be possible to obtain a competitive advantage by pursuing product differentiation—specifically, incorporating environmentally sound policies and practices into its **value chain** in order to create products that others did not have. Using principles of biomimicry (explained in chapter 3), and working in conjunction with a local forestry professor, CFP created Pure-Bond˚, a non-formaldehyde plywood. A first in the industry, PureBond® provided significant health benefits to CFP employees and customers by removing a known carcinogen from its products. With this, CFP became

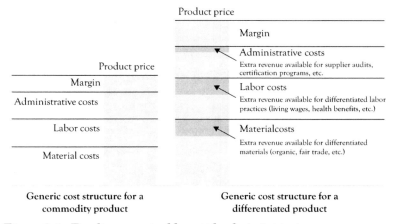

Figure 2.1. Funding sustainable supply chain initiatives.

the only producer in the industry that had a proprietary adhesive with greater bonding strength, better moisture resistance, and no off-gassing of formaldehyde, all without added cost to the customer.

When CFP first announced its intention to adopt formaldehyde-free resins, the plywood industry reacted with boycott threats and an extensive public relations campaign against CFP. They felt that by advertising a formaldehyde-free product, CFP was demonizing the gas. However, in early 2007, the California Air Resources Board enacted strict regulation focused on indoor air quality. Under the new regulations, manufacturers that continued to use formaldehyde-added resins in regulated products had to obtain third party certification demonstrating emissions standards compliance. With this regulation, CFP found itself in a very advantageous position. First, it was the only hardwood plywood company in the industry with a cost-competitive alternative to formaldehyde-based products. Second, it was the only company in the industry that could tell its customers not to worry about the new regulations; the price, availability, and performance of the company's products had been tested, whereas others' had not. With this, CFP was able to capture and retain considerable market share, as its competitors struggled to satisfy the regulations.[11]

In conclusion, it is important for a company to understand its competitive landscape before it embarks on a major sustainability initiative. How do the products in your market compete: on price or qualitative attributes? If you can pursue a differentiation strategy, what value attributes might you sell—or, how would you distinguish your company or your products from others'? If products compete on price alone, is there an opportunity to innovate in the market, and sell products that compete on a differentiated platform? If not, how can you manage your costs in a way that doesn't come at the expense of social and environmental goals, and in what other ways could you support a sustainability agenda (e.g., employee volunteer events)? And finally, for readers who are directly responsible for supply chain design and execution, what do all of these factors mean for your supply chain strategy?

These are central questions in the business development process— the back and forth dance of determining what business you want to be in, and how you might be successful in that business. The next section addresses the latter portion of this topic in more detail, specifically the utility of sustainable supply chain management in enabling competitive advantage and business success.

Achieving Competitive Advantage

The previous section laid out the basics of business strategy for readers unfamiliar with the topic, and indicated that a differentiated strategy is more suitable for pursuing goals related to social and environmental responsibility than a cost-focused strategy. However, not all companies that pursue differentiation also pursue sustainability. The question remains, then, as to why sustainability is a worthwhile pursuit from a competitive standpoint, and how sustainable supply chain management in particular contributes to competitive advantage.

Chapter 1 articulated many of the reasons that sustainability, in general, is a worthy business pursuit: enhanced marketability, deeper consumer loyalty and trust, unique and hard-to-replicate product designs, higher product prices, greater support for innovation and learning within the firm, and improved employee morale and productivity, to name a few. From a supply chain perspective, additional benefits include improved risk and threat management, the development of unique and hard-to-replicate supplier relationships, increased collaboration and communication among supply chain partners, and cost reductions resulting from ecoefficiencies.

In short, sustainable supply chain management uniquely positions companies to be aware of, adequately prepare for, and in some cases avoid many of today's supply chain risks and threats, such as resource scarcity and social and political instability. Likewise, a supply chain that is based on a collaborative, communicative, win-win premise is more likely to endure than one that is not, and it can assist companies with innovation, quality management, cost management, and risk management initiatives and processes. All of these factors contribute strongly to competitive advantage for companies with long supply chains.

An example of sustainable supply chain management contributing to competitive advantage can be seen in the U.S. children's toy industry, which was worth approximately $22 billion in 2008. This industry is characterized by intense rivalry, resulting from an abundance of product substitutes at the generic level (e.g., video games, books, candy) and at the product form level (e.g., thousands of versions of toy cars). Competition is therefore price-based, a characteristic encouraged by the fact that most parents see children's toys as short-term investments, at best. To manage costs in this environment, toy companies have shipped manufacturing jobs overseas. In 1993, the U.S. toy industry employed more than 42,000 factory workers; by 2007, manufacturing jobs in the industry had dropped to 17,000. By 2007, 85% of children's toys purchased in the United States were made in China.[12]

The outsourcing of toy production to countries with diminished environmental controls has resulted in an explosion of safety concerns for parents. Forty-five million toys were recalled in 2007 due to concerns over lead paint, magnets, and other safety hazards. In response, legislation was passed in 2008 to improve toy safety. The Consumer Product Safety Improvement Act of 2008 mandated factory-to-store tracking labels that could help with product recalls, dropped allowable lead limits in toys, dropped allowable phthalate limits in toy plastics, and mandated product safety testing.[13]

As many toy companies struggle to meet these new product design and supply chain mandates, one company is soaring past them. Green Toys, Inc. is a California-based toy manufacturer founded in 2007 on the premise of providing children and parents with fun, safe, and environmentally friendly products. All of the company's toys are made of recycled milk jugs, procured from municipal waste recyclers who collect the jugs curbside in California. Because the plastic is already food safe, Green Toys' products contain no toxins that create product safety concerns. The lack of external coatings also means the toys have no risk of lead contamination. Packaging, too, is environmentally friendly, made of recycled corrugated boxes with no plastic twist-ties or cellophane, making it easily recyclable. All of the company's manufacturing is done in the United States in a small geographical area near Mill Valley, which minimizes transportation miles during production. Third-party testing has verified the safety of Green Toys' products, and the sustainability of the company's supply chain—the company says it has reused over 10 million milk jugs to date—has given Green Toys considerable marketing cachet. The firm has won a number of product awards and generated significant press since its founding, and its annual growth rate each year has been 70%, despite the recession.[14]

Clearly, sustainable supply chain management can contribute strongly to competitive advantage, by both reducing threats and risks, and by increasing marketability. To help readers conceptualize the utility of sustainable supply chain management in their own firms, the next and final section of this chapter presents a strategic planning workshop, which can be used by companies to evaluate the depth of their overarching interest in sustainability, and create an authentic foundation for operationalizing their ideals. Further guidance in crafting the sustainable supply chain is offered in the remaining chapters of this book.

Strategic Planning Workshop

All businesses make decisions. To ensure a business makes decisions that align with its core purpose, it is necessary to define that purpose, and to create a clear "roadmap" that can keep the company on track as it pursues its purpose. This is the essence of a **strategic plan**. The primary components of a strategic plan are vision, mission, and value statements; a set of objectives articulating what the company wants to achieve with regard to its vision, mission, and values; strategies that will work the company toward its objectives; and action plans. Examples of these components are provided throughout the section, to guide readers as they use this workshop.

Beyond these basic components, strategic plans vary considerably, as do the processes used to create them. For example, a large, established company may develop a formal strategic plan, complete with planning teams and an outside facilitator, a multi month process, and a well-designed, visually appealing document as a deliverable. In contrast, the strategic plan for a startup may be developed by one person (e.g., the founder), during the course of one visioning session (e.g., while having a beer), with only slight documentation to relay the concept to other audiences (e.g., scribbles on a napkin). The ideas and basic strategies sketched out in such a "plan" would later be transitioned into a formal **business plan**, which more deeply examines the revenue side of things (markets, products, pricing, channels), the cost side of things (the value chain and its associated cost structure), and potential profits and cash flows.

Despite these variations, there is general agreement that the best strategic plans are those that exist "in the body," meaning all members of an organization are so connected to a company's vision, mission, values, and goals that their actions simply reflect the plan in motion. Likewise, good strategic plans offer enough guidance to keep an organization centered and on course, but are flexible enough that new opportunities and challenges can be addressed in stride. This can be a difficult balance to strike, because a good strategic plan must also be implementable, meaning there aren't insurmountable internal or external constraints holding the plan back. Thus, while big-picture in nature, it is important to put a fair amount of mental work during a planning process toward how strategic ideas will be operationalized.

Strategic plans and planning processes tend to fail for a few common reasons. These include a lack of interest on the part of leadership to execute a new vision; an organizational culture that cannot embrace change; a lack of honesty on the part of participants about the true state of affairs of a company (financially or otherwise); the creation of a plan that doesn't have genuine buy in from participants, particularly those who are actually going to be implementing the plan and thus are best-positioned to inform strategic discussions; and the creation of a plan that isn't implementable due to insurmountable constraints. Planning processes can also fail if they get beleaguered by company politics, or drag on interminably.

In short, successful strategic planning requires a company to be efficient, honest, thorough, creative, and bold, and top leadership must be committed to the process and to implementation. Without these prerequisites, it is not worth investing time or money in strategic planning.

Strategic Planning Steps

There is no one right way to create a strategic plan, and no one format that a strategic plan should take; the best plan development process is whatever works for the company at hand. That being said, the following process is fairly common and provides a good starting point for the business or entrepreneur that wants to articulate a clear sense of purpose, and create a clear roadmap to achieve that purpose. In each of the steps suggested below, ideas or concerns unique to the social and environmentally responsible business are noted; Step 5 also specifically discusses the creation of a sustainable supply chain strategy:

- Step 1: Invite the right people to participate
- Step 2: Develop vision, mission, and value statements
- Step 3: Create compelling objectives
- Step 4: Conduct an environmental scan
- Step 5: Clarify strategic options and craft strategies
- Step 6: Develop action plans (not always applicable)
- Step 7: Implement

Step 1: Invite the Right People to Participate

Good planning requires that the right stakeholders be involved at the right time; "stakeholders" are those who will be materially impacted by a plan, and those who will play a substantial role in its success. Owners and top managers should most certainly be involved in strategic planning, as should selected members of the board. Some line employees might also be invited into the process, if they are important to the future of the organization, or gifted in their understanding of strategic and operational issues. Note that caution should be used in inviting employees if fundamental changes to a business are likely. The concern about an organizational redesign and layoffs can greatly influence the ability of some participants to think objectively about a business' future, for obvious and good reason.

Overall, the planning team should be balanced: visionaries and pragmatists; board members, executives, top managers, and line employees; those with a deep understanding of a company's past (particularly if there is a need to communicate radically new ideas in the "language" of older stakeholders), and those with a keen sense of where a company might want to go. Key partners might also be invited, if their involvement in the new idea is anticipated to be vital; this includes the heads of interested NGOs, if relevant. The right size for a strategic planning team will vary. The smaller the team, the smoother the process. At the same time, a team that is too small may not adequately represent an organization's context or needs, and as a result, may create a plan that lacks viability or buy in from those tasked with implementation.

Note that it can be difficult for companies to maintain objectivity during planning. Hesitancy to admit difficult realities is common. Overzealous participants can also challenge planning. Lastly, the presence of company power holders can be very intimidating for team members with less power (e.g., line staff). Therefore, it can be worth the money to invite an experienced facilitator to guide the strategic planning process—someone who is removed from company politics and power imbalances, who has nothing to gain or lose from the outcome of a process, and who is therefore inclined to treat insights and contributions equally and push for objectivity.

Step 2: Develop Vision, Mission, and Value Statements

Once you have your team assembled, and have identified the parameters of your process (roles and responsibilities, how long you want the process to take, points in the process at which you will float your ideas with people outside of the planning team to get input and direction, etc.), it is time to develop vision, mission, and value statements.

Defining a vision is essentially defining a desired future state for your world, your community, the people you want to serve, etc. A mission statement articulates what your company will do to achieve that vision. There is no rule that says a company must have both a vision and mission; many companies have a combination of the two that they simply term their "mission," and this is fine. However, thinking through your vision can help in the creation of a mission statement.

Examples of general questions to ask during vision and mission development include:

- What possibilities are you passionate about? Why do these possibilities excite you?
- What issues are you deeply concerned about? What about these issues concerns you?
- What is needed to achieve your vision, or the address the concerns you've identified?
- How can your company best contribute to the achievement or the solution?

Note that although in-depth research on your company's operating environment will occur in a later stage of work, being able to have an informed discussion about the sustainability aspects of your vision and mission necessitates that your planning team have some baseline knowledge of the social and environmental issues that exist in your industry. Questions to consider therefore, which will influence everything from visioning to supply chain planning, include:

- How are products in your industry typically made? Where are they made? Is there a deep need for manual labor? Are there unique ways you can address labor needs and constraints? Are there ways you can utilize labor to achieve a social good?
- What natural resources are used in your industry? What is the state of those resources: are they abundant, scarce,

or threatened? How can your company avoid furthering problems related to resource overuse?

- What emissions or byproducts are typically created in your industry? Are they inevitable or can they be minimized via better product design, process design, or logistics practices?
- What level of consumer waste is typically generated in your industry? Can it be minimized? What kind of consumer waste is generated? Could this waste be reutilized in some way?

As vision and mission statements develop, aim for pithiness. One sentence for each should suffice. Thus, the debate about what should go into these statements is likely to be robust and may take a fair amount of time. Ideally, once crafted, your vision and mission statements should last you a long time, rarely needing revision. In this, a vision statement in particular is intended to be aspirational and motivational, versus measurable and quickly achieved. Examples include:

- "A just and prosperous clean energy future" (Focus the Nation, vision statement);
- "To bring inspiration and innovation to every athlete* in the world. (*'If you have a body, you are an athlete')." (Nike, mission statement).

As vision and mission statements develop, the team should also track the principles that repeatedly surface during discussion—or, the company's values. These, too, should be honed into a short list of guiding principles that the company follows, completing the conceptual framework that a company adheres to as it conducts its work.

Note that although a company's vision and mission are ideally fully understood by all of its employees, and thus useful in everyday decision-making, they can often be too abstract to serve this purpose. If this is the case, value statements can be a useful stand-in when employees need to make daily, independent choices that support a company's core purpose. In this, organizational behavior can also be a great sign of the values that a company truly holds; people behave as they are incentivized to behave, not as a company instructs them to act. If your organization's culture does not reflect the values your company wants to hold, you need to reconsider your company's incentive framework—that is, its system of formal rewards (promotions, raises, bonuses) and informal rewards (recognition).

Step 3: Create Compelling Objectives

After vision and mission statements are developed, objectives need to be created. Objectives should be clear and measurable, and directly tied to mission achievement. Sustainably focused companies will therefore want to create objectives that directly address the positive impact they seek to achieve via their operations, in addition to financial objectives. Hypothetical examples include:

- "Give away 10 million shoes to children in need within five years."
- "Become the market leader of environmentally friendly toys in the U.S. in three years."
- "Launch the first residential hardware line made of 100% scrap metal in two years."
- "Become the U.S. market leader in sustainable food service and catering in three years."

Generally, only a few objectives are created for a strategic plan (three to five is a good range). Objectives should be attainable, but only after a sustained and dedicated effort spanning several years. In this, they should directly influence how resources in a firm are allocated; they are the first stage of operationalizing the mission.

Step 4: Conduct an Environmental Scan

After vision, mission, and value statements have been articulated, and objectives drafted, a company needs to craft an understanding of three basic things: its external operating environment; its internal condition; and its most viable competitive approach, given its unique external and internal situation. To do this, an environmental scan should be conducted.

Many research methods can be used to develop an environmental scan, such as focus groups, stakeholder interviews, and employee surveys. Whatever your technique, you should design your research program and tools in a way that will help your company gather objective data. For instance, managers should not expect to get objective input about a company's weaknesses via direct interviews with line employees.

One way to help frame the results of an environmental scan is to create a "SWOT" or, a summary of your company's Strengths, Weaknesses, Opportunities, and Threats; an example SWOT is shown in Table 2.2 for a hypothetical food service and catering company that is contemplating a sustainable ingredient sourcing initiative. Additionally, a more comprehensive, written summary of findings should be developed. This document should be discussed by the planning team to reach a general consensus about the company's operating context and its most likely source(s) of competitive advantage.

We emphasize this need for discussion, revision, and agreement. This is one of the most important actions a company can take to set the stage for strategic success. It compels a deep understanding of a company's existing position and potential, forcing a team to address difficult truths and realities head-on. The success that a planning team feels when it

Table 2.2. Example SWOT for large food service/catering company considering sustainable ingredient sourcing program.

Strengths	Weaknesses
• Great rapport with current clients; may make it easier to take risks, make early mistakes	• No experience developing ingredient-specific food sourcing policies.
• Internal staff have expressed a desire to be more innovative in their jobs, and to create the "next great thing"	• No experience developing local food supply chain: contracting, delivery, etc.; currently reliant on large distributors for ingredients
• Good basic business systems in place; can support risk taking in supply chain	• Kitchen staff have no means to share menu ideas and assist with creativity
Opportunities	**Threats**
• Clients are looking for ways to differentiate themselves; we can assist them in achieving their own goals	• Several main players already established in the sustainable food service and catering industry: can we grow?
• More revenue for clients means more lucrative contracts for us	• Best local and organic suppliers may already be "taken" by competitors: can we get good products consistently?
• Growth in organic food sector is exploding; sustainable supply chain may be getting easier to implement	• Smaller suppliers may be less reliable and have more expensive food

finally agrees on a company's state of affairs can also be cathartic, providing great clarity and momentum for the rest of the strategy development process, and for implementation.

To guide research and discussion, a number of sustainability-focused prompt questions are listed below. These should be explored in addition to more general business topics.

Consumers, competitors, and rivalry:

- What consumer need does your company address? Consider the value of your company's vision and mission to consumers, in addition to the value of your products and services.
- What is the degree of rivalry in your industry? Are there a lot of competitors, or just a few?
- On what basis do companies in your industry compete (e.g., price, quality, etc.)?

  - If products compete only on the basis of price, do you see a unique opportunity to disrupt the market by selling a differentiated product or service? Who would buy this, and why?
  - If products compete on a differentiated basis, what is so unique about your company, product, or service that a consumer might want to buy from you?

- Is there a substantial benefit to being a first mover in your market? If so, what will prevent someone from replicating your success? Or, should you be replicating someone else?
- How do green or socially responsible companies in your industry measure and convey their achievements, in relation to their goals? Can their claims be verified? If not, what does that mean for your company, product, or service? If so, what does that also mean for you?
- How does your organizational structure affect your ability to compete? For example, if you are a social entrepreneur, what brand image benefits might you receive? What costs might this structure also entail? How will your structure compare to that of your competitors?

- If you are an existing company, do you have past indiscretions that will hinder your ability to compete? Additionally, have the root causes of those issues been addressed?

Regulatory, political, and economic factors:

- What regulatory and political factors exist or are surfacing in your industry? Are you aligned with those regulations or out of alignment with them?
- Will regulatory and political factors help create a market for your product or service, or might they close down or negatively alter the markets in which you are operating?
- Will the creation of sustainability standards, via regulation, help you compete? Or, will it make it easier for others to copy your process and thus degrade your competitive advantage?
- How sensitive will your products or services be to economic ups and downs?
- Are there sustainability incentives on the horizon that could stimulate market demand (e.g., tax credits)? Are your product or service concepts in line with those incentives?

Leadership and organizational culture:

- Do you have a leader who will keep employees passionate, energized, and enthusiastic?
- Do you have a leader or advisory team that can keep the company on financial track?
- Is the entire management team aware of and on board with the new direction?
- How will your new direction be communicated to stakeholders not engaged in the planning process? How will you encourage them to be strong supporters of the vision and mission?
- Will your organizational culture support your company's vision and mission? Are your incentives structured to promote behavior that aligns with your vision, mission, and values?

Investment, ownership, and growth:

- Do you have the facilities, equipment, and technology you need to launch your concept? Are there ways to lessen the upfront costs of your venture; that is, make it incremental in nature?
- Do you have talented, knowledgeable people on board to help you build out your idea? What do you need to give these people to be a part of your venture? Where will you find them?
- Who might invest in your idea? What will they want in exchange for their investment? When will they want to exit? Will their ownership negatively influence your vision and mission?
- Do you aspire to be a public company, or to sell to another company? How might that benefit or hinder your vision and mission?
- How big do you want your company to ultimately be? Will growth positively or negatively impact your vision and mission?

Note that because your company's strategies will be a unique response to your company's operating context, it is advisable to find a way to make environmental scanning an integral part of your firm's management process. Having continuously current knowledge about the factors influencing your firm's success is key to knowing if, when, and how to change your strategic approach.

Step 5: Clarify Strategic Options and Craft Strategies

Once a company has a strong grasp on its operating context, it needs to decide how to best pursue its vision, mission, and objectives. Clearly, the previous discussion of strategy applies here, and at this point a company should have a strong awareness of the general approach that will best suit its needs given its operating environment. However, strategy development requires more than just a definition of the "what." Crafting ideas about *how* to successfully differentiate your company in the cluttered field of sustainable business, or *how* to be a cost leader that successfully pursues authentic social or environmental objectives, will give your company far more guidance as it proceeds than simply choosing one generic approach over another.

To develop "how" concepts, the results of the environmental scan need to be drawn upon. Your team should have a keen sense of where market opportunities exist and what it takes to be successful in your industry. This knowledge should be matched up with your team's honest assessment of what it does well and what it does not do well. Based on this analysis, you should end up with a shortlist of the most targeted actions your company can take in the next few years to achieve its objectives. Example strategies are listed in Table 2.3.

Note that while strategies are inherently integrated in nature—drawing on all of the operational elements of a company to craft a short list of ideas about mission achievement—the strategy development process is a good time for supply chain managers to think specifically about their firm's supply chain strategy. As noted earlier, different supply chain strategies are appropriate for different business goals—lean and physically efficient supply chains work best for firms that are striving to be cost leaders, and responsive, agile supply chains work best for firms that want to sell on a differentiated platform. In addition, firms interested in sustainability are going to want to prioritize social and environmental considerations in supply chain design and execution.

Table 2.3. Strategy Example for Large Food Service/Catering Company

Objective 1: Become the U.S. market leader in sustainable food service and catering in three years
• *Strategy 1*: Specialize in seasonal, region-specific menus that highlight organic and locally grown ingredients, and are a major draw for the high-value customers our clients want to bring in • *Strategy 2*: Become an acknowledged innovator in zero waste in our industry, diverting as much food waste, used cooking oil, and other food production materials away from landfills as possible at the facilities in which we work (good for our reputation, good for our clients' reputations) • *Strategy 3*: Develop expertise in about how to sustainably manage the food and entertainment facilities in which we work (an added value for clients)

Issues to consider when developing a sustainable supply chain strategy therefore include:

- The physical layout of your supply chain structure
- The adequacy of the processes that keep goods flowing through that structure
- The adequacy of the systems that support those processes (e.g., supplier incentive systems)
- The nature and depth of existing and potential supply chain partnerships
- Opportunities for supply chain participants to gain knowledge and continually innovate
- The flexibility of the supply chain to adapt to disruption and change.[15]

All told, your supply chain strategy needs to align with and reflect your business strategy. If your business's strategy is to be a cost leader, you need a supply chain strategy that delivers on efficiency goals, not differentiation concepts. Likewise, if your business wants to be sustainable, you need a supply chain that is aware of and responds to social and environmental priorities, in addition to more standard differentiation needs related to responsiveness and flexibility.

Step 6: Develop Action Plans (Not Always Applicable)

Creating action plans is a semi-optional step in strategic planning. That is, large companies tend to have well-developed work planning processes that connect overarching business strategy to operational strategies and tasks; these processes, then, comprise action planning. However, small companies may lack such processes, in which case they will want to develop action items within their strategic plan. Action plans consist of short-term goals and implementation steps, often spanning only a year's time. As they are tactical in nature, they should be completed by functional area managers who control the allocation of resources in a firm. Ideally, these managers were also involved in the larger strategic planning effort, so that the strategic intent of the business, overall, can be made manifest in daily operations.

Table 2.4 shows the basic structure and components of an action plan, building on the example from Table 2.3. The action plan includes a restatement of the specific objective and strategy being addressed, and articulates the actions needed to carry out the strategy. It also identifies what department is responsible for the action step, and by when it needs to be done. Note that when this strategy is broken down, the depth of its impact on all operational departments in the company is actually quite significant.

Table 2.4. Action Plan Example for Large Food Service/Catering Company

Objective 1: Become the U.S. market leader in sustainable food service and catering in three years*		
Supporting Strategy 1: Specialize in seasonal, region-specific menus that highlight organic and locally grown ingredients, and are a major draw for the high-value customers our clients want to bring in		
Actions required to carry out strategy	**Leader?**	**Deadline?**
• Develop ingredient-specific food sourcing policies to guide exec chefs in menu design and supplier relationship development	Kitchen	
• Conduct training with exec chefs to ensure they understand the principles, policies, and techniques of sustainable food sourcing	Purchasing	
• Create a feedback loop to get input from chefs regarding changes and improvements to the sourcing policies	Human Resources	
• Create an information forum for chefs to share menu concepts, supplier development tips, etc.	IT	
• Meet with national distributors to ascertain the depth and value of their "green" and "organic" food products lists	Purchasing	
• Refine cost management approaches given changes to food buying and sourcing practices; track food costs carefully	Accounting	
• Revisit incentive structure for head chefs and kitchen teams to ensure informal and formal bonuses align with innovation and sourcing goals	Exec Team	

*Note: Some sort of metric would typically be developed to track progress toward the objective over time (e.g., market share, annual sales, etc.).

Step 7: Implement

Some companies fail to achieve objectives because their strategies are poorly designed; others fail because good strategies are poorly implemented. To encourage good implementation, the following should be ensured:

- *Employees clearly understand the plan and their role in making implementation successful.* A formal rollout for a new plan may be worthwhile; training may also be needed.
- *Employee incentives match the plan's objectives.* For example, if bonuses are tied solely to cost cutting, it may be hard to encourage action on sustainability goals.
- *Processes and the managerial will exist to ensure accountability.* In addition to having incentives tied to business objectives, review processes should be tied to objectives at every level. If performance is insufficient, action should be taken to ascertain the root cause of the problem, and fix it.
- *Methods exist for employees to productively question and improve the content of the plan.* Employee questions about plan content should be allowed and encouraged; after all, your business isn't what you say you do, it's what your employees actually do. Use a plan launch as an opportunity to become aligned.
- *Methods exist to communicate your achievements to the outside world.* Others should know what your firm is achieving, as a means to enhance your market position and pay for your endeavors, and to prove to others that substantial social and environmental responsibility initiatives can be accomplished.

Conclusion

Operational strategies must align with overarching business strategy in order for both to be effective. Working with this knowledge, this chapter assessed the connection between business strategy, supply chain strategy, and sustainability. We examined the generic business strategies of cost leadership and differentiation to see how they influence a company's ability to pursue robust sustainability initiatives like sustainable supply chain management. In this, we concluded that differentiation is a preferred strategy for companies interested in sustainability, as it gives companies more financial room to create flexible and responsive supply chains, and to make structural, procedural, and systemic decisions that support social and environmental goals in supply chain management. We also reviewed how sustainable supply chain management can be a contributor to a company's competitive advantage, helping with risk aversion and mitigation, and encouraging the development of strong internal competencies. We concluded with a strategic planning workshop, which walked readers through the development of a strategic plan. The remainder of this book now presents the techniques and tools of sustainable supply chain management, from product and process design to product end-of-life management.

Checklist

To assist with applying ideas from this chapter, consider:

- Do you or does your company have the passion and leadership required to be a successful and enduring business? Do you have the agility and ability to make sound compromises that are often required of sustainable businesses?
- Does the industry in which you are operating have room for a differentiated business? If you must pursue a cost leadership strategy, how can you incorporate sustainability ideas into your business operations?
- How might sustainable supply chain management play a role in your business' success? What will it help you address, or how can it help you achieve a competitive advantage?
- Do you have a strategic plan, or at least a general strategic framework that can serve as a roadmap to accomplishing your vision, mission, and objectives?

Recommended Readings and Videos

- Mycoskie, Blake (2011). *Start Something that Matters.* This book is a light, easy read that can help entrepreneurial readers think about their passion and how it can translate into sustainable business success.
- William James Foundation (www.williamjamesfoundation.org). The William James Foundation manages socially responsible business plan competitions, handing out $100,000 in prize money annually. Even if you are not interested in competing, the foundation's website has superior information about factors to consider when launching a sustainable business.
- Patagonia. *The Footprint Chronicles.* (http://www.patagonia.com/us/footprint/index.jsp). A great overview of sustainable supply chain management in action. Allows readers to trace products through Patagonia's supply chain, and provides informational videos that examine strategic, tactical, moral, and environmental issues in supply chain management.

CHAPTER 3

Sustainable Product and Process Design

Consumer demand for sustainable products is increasing worldwide. In fact, one 2009 study—which surveyed consumers in nine countries and interviewed shoppers in seven Chinese cities—concluded that consumers today are buying more "green" products than ever before, particularly those that are also considered to be of high quality. Shoppers also want producers to be completely transparent, have good environmental records, be clear about product risks and safety, provide information about products' environmental impacts, have high ethical standards, and treat employees fairly. The study, conducted by the Boston Consulting Group, also reported that many executives at leading consumer products companies today now agree that differentiated green products provide additional market share and bring down the costs of value chains—significant insights given current economic conditions.[1]

Consumer categories like paper and packaged products, disposable home products, fresh meat and vegetables, electronics, and appliances present particularly large opportunities for innovative companies to develop and sell green, ethical, and sustainable products. Ingestible products such as food and beverages lead the pack in sustainable product category growth, in part because sustainability has become synonymous with quality in this realm. For example, in Europe, more than 75% of consumers make food purchases based on sustainability standards, and 30% try a product for the first time based on its ethical value.[2] Other fast-growing sustainable product categories include building products, sustainable energy production products, and energy and resource reduction technologies.

Given these trends, companies that focus on sustainability need to learn how to develop products that meet common sustainability standards, improve existing products to meet these standards, and enhance the processes they use to create and deliver products—that is, their supply chain. As we will find in chapter 5, companies focused on sustainability also need to contemplate the relationship between product design and product end-of-life management, ensuring that product designs are compatible with reuse and recycling infrastructure. This chapter aims to meet these needs, giving readers a description of the primary techniques and tools used in sustainable product and process design, development, and improvement.

Process and Product Frameworks and Tools

Every product's supply chain is simply a bundle of processes, from buying raw materials, services and other inputs, to transforming those inputs into **value-added** products, to the final distribution and marketing of outputs. In addition to desired outputs, by-products are often generated in a production process, some of which have positive value, like scrap metal, paper, and heat, while others have negative value, like contaminants, worker accidents, and emissions and other waste. Information about the resulting product's conformance to company and consumer expectations is an additional output. This information can be used as feedback to improve a product and a process over time. A generic process is illustrated in Figure 3.1.

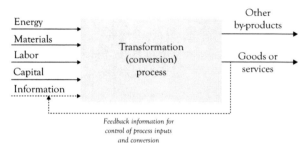

Figure 3.1. Inputs, outputs, and feedback.

Many frameworks have evolved over time to analyze sustainability issues in company processes, as shown in Figure 3.2.[3] In the early stages of environmental concern (1970s), most companies took a reactive stance toward pollution control, with a focus on regulatory compliance and cleanup technologies. From a process perspective, this "end of pipe" approach focused solely on output (pollution). By the 1980s, the focus had shifted to the inputs and conversion steps of a process—or, efforts to prevent pollution from occurring. Here, companies examined ways to improve operational efficiency and minimize waste (both resource and pollution), which typically aligned with quality management programs. By the 1990s, multiple frameworks and tools had emerged for process improvement and sustainable design, including eco-efficiency, design for the environment, The Natural Step, and industrial ecology. More recently, cradle to cradle, life cycle assessment, and biomimicry frameworks have influenced product and process design activities. These methods are all discussed in detail below.

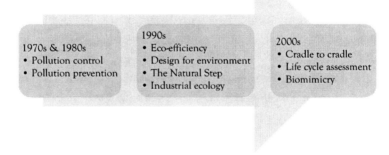

Figure 3.2. Environmental product and process frameworks.

Eco-Efficiency

Eco-efficiencies aim to reduce resource inputs and processing steps, minimize waste and toxic product use, and maximize the desired outputs of a process. Consequently, costs are reduced and overall productivity and margins improve. One of the most useful tools to support ecoefficiency efforts is the **value stream map**.

Value Stream Mapping

Value stream mapping is a type of analysis in which designers reconstruct a particular process on paper and then determine if each step in the process is adding value to the entity under review, or simply generating waste. The goal of the map is to lay out the steps of an existing or proposed process, gather relevant data regarding each step of the process, and eliminate or reduce steps that are not adding value from a customer or sustainable stakeholder's perspective—such as wasted materials, natural resources, labor, worker's health, and so forth.

The key steps of mapping are to identify: (a) the entity under review, such as an item, an order, a customer, a proposal, a policy, or any object or concept that passes through a series of process steps; (b) clear boundaries, such as starting and ending points, and lines of demarcation between the customer, the order, and other relevant information flows; and (c) the resource measurements relevant to the process's improvement. It is important that map creators keep it simple and consider whether a specific detail adds any insight—that is, whether or not it is necessary to map every condition of an entity's process, or simply a selected array of conditions.

The mapping exercise typically starts on a large scale (e.g., manufacturing a car body) but then quickly breaks down into sub-processes (e.g., metal fabrication, part coating, assembly, welding, and so on). Next, a key resource or set of resources is chosen for examination and review (e.g., water use, energy use, hazardous waste, labor, percentage local content, etc.), and each step is measured for the amount of resource consumed at that step. At each step, the relevant resources required by the step, and the step's subsequent waste outputs, are listed as illustrated in Figure 3.3 for a parts manufacturing facility. Finally, the percentage of value-added versus non-value-added activity is calculated for each step, using the classifications summarized below.

Figure 3.3. Value stream map: Resource inputs and outputs.

Value-added activities: These activities add a desired function, form, or feature to a product or service, better meeting consumer expectations or enabling a competitive advantage (e.g., more environmentally friendly, locally produced, fair trade, reduced price, faster delivery, better quality, etc.). In short, these are activities that a customer or stakeholder would be willing to pay for.

Business non-value-added activities: These are activities that a customer or stakeholder doesn't want to pay for (it does not increase value in their eyes), but are required for some reason. Examples include accounting, legal, and regulatory activities, like customs inspections that are required by law. Some tasks reduce potential financial liabilities or risk at a company, like the inspection and testing of artificial heart valves, or climbing harnesses, prior to their shipment. Alternatively, some tasks are required for certification, or required by financial review entities like the IRS. Finally, an entire process could break down if a certain task is removed. Any of these are examples that would be classified as a business non-value-added activity.

Waste non-value-added activities: Waste activities do not add value in the eyes of the consumer or stakeholder, nor are they essential to a business's functioning in any manner. From a sustainability perspective, any resource waste (e.g., the gap between water used versus water actually needed in a process) or hazardous condition or material is non-value-added. From a productivity perspective, rework is waste, as are excesses in any necessary business activity—such as excessive setup, inspecting, counting, handling, transporting, moving, storing, copying, signing, etc.

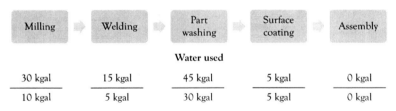

Summary of water waste
Water used: 95,000 gallons
Actual water needed: 50,000 gallons
Water wasted: 45,000 gallons

Milling	Welding	Part washing	Surface coating	Assembly

Water used

30 kgal	15 kgal	45 kgal	5 kgal	0 kgal
10 kgal	5 kgal	30 kgal	5 kgal	0 kgal

Actual water needed

Figure 3.4. Water used vs. water needed.

After all the mapped steps have been classified, designers then target areas where non-value-added activities are occurring and attempt to eliminate or minimize the waste. For example, continuing with our previous map and probing further into the use of water resources, Figure 3.4 provides the actual measurement of water use compared to the water needed at each step of a parts manufacturing process. With this map, the wasted water is displayed and the improvement team can focus on the problematic steps—milling, welding, and parts washing—to achieve improvement.

Value stream mapping can serve an array of product and process improvement objectives, depending on a company's strategy. Thus, one can measure many process factors using this technique, as noted in Table 3.1. For example, companies striving to be environmentally conscious while maintaining low production costs could have material use measurements in place at each stage of a process under review. Working to improve this metric will help minimize material waste going to landfills, while also reducing disposal costs.

In short, a value stream map is a useful tool for identifying process steps needing improvement, in order to reduce non-value-added activities. As shown in Figure 3.5, waste can come from many sources, allowing innovative thinkers to conceptualize many unique and creative solutions to waste, like reinventing a product or considering different market segments for a revised eco-product. All elements become fair game for change, including raw materials, product design, job design, processing steps used, information systems and technology, equipment or tools, and suppliers. Really, anything but customers may be changed, unless the

Table 3.1. Value Stream Mapping Measurement Ideas

Factors	Measurement
Quality	Key product or service characteristic of interest: mistakes, failures, complaints, returned items, repairs, time, etc.
Material	Materials that go into the product or service at different steps: components, packaging, paper, solvent, resin, paints, water, etc.
Cost	Time, expenses, and labor at each step.
Delivery	Things that impact delivery of the product or services to customer: shortages, defaults in payment, delays, or wait time.
Energy resources	kWh or BTUs, miles per gallon, etc.
Innovation	Number of radically new or incremental improved products introduced.
Local content	Materials or labor content in process step produced in regions of importance.
Safety	Accidents, mistakes, breakdowns.
3 Rs	Use of recycled, renewable, and reused materials.
Understanding and usability	Meeting the needs, expectations, and satisfaction level of the customers.

Source: Author.

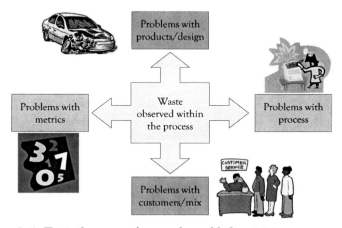

Figure 3.5. Typical causes of non-value-added activities.

customers themselves do not add value—for example, a different customer segment might match the product better or pay for the ethical and environmentally enhanced product a company wishes to produce.

Example: Nike's Toxicity and Waste Reduction Efforts

In the late 1990s, Nike set out to eliminate waste and toxicity in its products as part of its official sustainability policy. The company knew that using alternative materials could reduce worker health problems and other environmental issues, in addition to improving Nike's brand image and product appeal. One of Nike's initial steps in operationalizing this idea was to develop a positive list of substances to be used in manufacturing in addition to targeting negative or toxic substances such as polyvinyl chloride (PVC). By mapping its processes for footwear and non-screen-print apparel manufacturing, Nike's designers were able to identify sources of waste and toxic substance use in this aspect of its production process.

Working with its manufacturing partners and chemical suppliers, Nike reduced its use of organic solvents by 88% (saving $4.5 million in raw materials), substituted water-based cements into 90% of its shoes, which saved the company from using 1.6 million gallons of solvents per year, and redesigned its shoe box, saving an additional 4,000 tons of raw materials and $1.6 million annually. By 2004, none of Nike's apparel and only 2% of its shoes contained PVC. The 2% remaining in its shoes fell under the business non-value-added category, since the shoes had performance and price requirements that were obstacles to the development of an alternative. Nike also made great progress with an environmentally preferable rubber formulation that reduced toxic chemical use and greenhouse gases in its shoes.[4]

Workshop: Value Stream Mapping

1. Do a generalized map of a process at home or at work, starting with its major functional steps (select a process with fewer than 15 sub processes).
2. Decide on two relevant metrics (one should be sustainability-oriented; another could be the major operational focus of the company, such as cost, quality, flexibility, etc.).

(Continued)

3. Pick one of the major steps, and explode it into its specific steps (aim for fewer than 20).

4. Evaluate value-added (V), business non-value-added (B), and waste non-value-added activities (N). Justify your categorizations.

5. Answer the following questions:

    a. What percentage of the steps are non-value added (i.e., 3 *N*/20 total = 15%)?

    b. What proportion of each type of measure could be improved (i.e., [actual water use–minimum water required]/total water use)?

    c. How would you modify the non-value-added activities that do not align with your mission?

    d. Show the opportunity areas and potential innovations.

Design for the Environment

The **Design for the Environment** (DfE) framework considers the complete environmental and health impact of a product or process, from material extraction to disposal. There are two main activities that comprise DfE: **Quality Function Deployment for the Environment** (QFDE) and Life Cycle Assessment (LCA), as shown in Figure 3.6.[5]

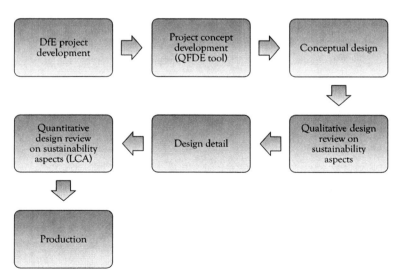

Figure 3.6. DfE flow and support tools.

In QFDE, an organization commits to creating or improving a product so that it has better sustainability performance. QFDE utilizes and builds on the more baseline Quality Function Deployment (QFD) tool, which is a long-standing quality improvement tool used to identify consumer requirements and bring them to the fore during a product's design process. For DfE, the requirements of the sustainability-oriented consumer are what matters, in addition to the requirements of other sustainability stakeholders, like recyclers, policymakers, government, society, the environment at large, and so forth. QFDE is used to translate the needs of these stakeholders (their "voices") into appropriate product design features.

Next, a design concept is developed, which is assessed qualitatively for its sustainability performance. If it does not meet approval during design review, the concept is modified until the concept passes design review. After refinement, a detailed design is developed, and LCA is used to quantitatively assess the design's sustainability impact. Again, the design could be tweaked or adjusted for better LCA numbers at this point. Finally, the design goes into production.

QFDE and LCA are described in more detail below, with illustrative examples to help show how these activities work. The two tools can be used together or independently depending on the needs of the organization.

Quality Function Deployment for the Environment

For the typical QFD process, four stages of work exist: (a) defining design or engineering requirements; (b) parts deployment; (c) process planning; and (d) production planning.[6] For the purposes of this book, we will focus on the first stage of work only, from the environmental perspective: determining engineering metrics for optimal product sustainability.

This stage of work begins by generating a list of customer requirements or needs (CNs), as illustrated in Figure 3.7 for a moss removal product. The CN list is generated via stakeholder focus groups. The CNs touch on all the needs important to stakeholders, including cost, quality, and sustainability performance requirements. Each CN is given a stakeholder rating (e.g., 1 to 9, with 9 being the most important need; these ratings

Row #	Weight chart	Relative weight	Customer importance	Customer needs
1	▨	15%	6	Little or NO PPE*
2	▨	15%	2	Less time
3	▨	15%	5	Easy to apply and wash
4	▨	10%	4	Low cost
5	▨	10%	2	Low environmental impact
6	▨	20%	7	No impact on surface being treated
7	▨	25%	8	Removes moss completely

Personal protective equipment

Figure 3.7. Customer needs, roof moss removal product.

are developed by the stakeholders). Each need is then also given a relative weight (totaling 100%; the weightings are developed by the design team). As you can see, there is a mix of functional and environmental needs represented in the example, from moss removal performance, cost, and time, to the need for personal protective equipment (PPE) during application, to the environmental impact of the product.

Engineering metrics (EMs) that relate to the environmental needs articulated during the CN identification process are then defined (Figure 3.8). These metrics are developed by the design and engineering team. A more extensive list of common environmental needs and associated engineering metrics is provided in Table 3.2, to give readers ideas about how a particular need might manifest into something measurable. Clearly, many environmental needs will have several metrics that could work as a measurement.

Next, the body of the QFDE "house" is built, the CNs comprising the left-hand wall of the house, and the EMs comprising the ceiling, as shown in Figure 3.9. This house shows the perceived relationship between the CNs and the EMs, as determined by the design team. One can see

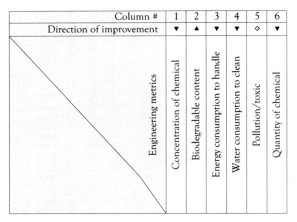

Figure 3.8. Engineering metrics, roof moss removal product.

Table 3.2. Sample of Environmental Needs and Engineering Metrics

Environmental need	Environmental engineering metric
Less material usage	Weight
Less energy and water consumption	Volume
Easy to transport and store	Number of parts
Easy to process and assemble	Variety of materials
High durability	Likelihood of getting dirty or oxidizing
Easy to reuse	Hardness
Easy to disassemble and sort	Physical lifetime
Easy to maintain	Energy consumption
Easy to compact	Rate of recycled material
Safe to incinerate	Sensory impact (noise, visual, etc.)
Easy to dispose of or safe to landfill	Emissions mass (air, water, soil)
Harmless to biosphere	Biodegradability
Safe emissions	Material toxicity

Source: Adapted from Masui et al. (2003).

that the CN "less time" correlates positively with the EM "concentration of chemical," indicating that as the chemical concentration increases in the product, the customer needs to apply it for less time. Likewise, the CN "easy to apply and wash" correlates negatively with the EM "biodegradable content," so as the product becomes easier to use, the less biodegradable content is in the product.

The roof of the house can be used to show the correlation between different EMs, as shown in Figure 3.10. As seen from the example, several

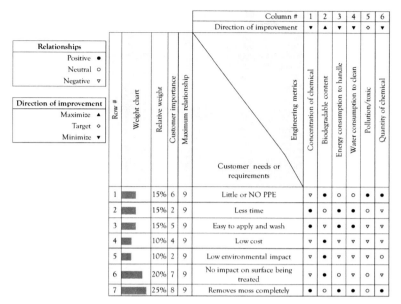

Relationships		
Positive	•	
Neutral	○	
Negative	▽	

Direction of improvement		
Maximize	▲	
Target	◇	
Minimize	▼	

Column #				1	2	3	4	5	6
Direction of improvement				▼	▲	▼	▼	◇	▼
Row # / Weight chart / Relative weight / Customer importance / Maximum relationship			Customer needs or requirements	Concentration of chemical	Biodegradable content	Energy consumption to handle	Water consumption to clean	Pollution/toxic	Quantity of chemical
1	15%	6	9	Little or NO PPE	▽	•	○	○	•	•
2	15%	2	9	Less time	•	○	•	•	○	▽
3	15%	5	9	Easy to apply and wash	•	▽	•	•	▽	▽
4	10%	4	9	Low cost	▽	•	▽	▽	▽	▽
5	10%	2	9	Low environmental impact	▽	•	▽	▽	▽	○
6	20%	7	9	No impact on surface being treated	▽	•	○	▽	○	▽
7	25%	8	9	Removes moss completely	•	○	•	•	○	•

Figure 3.9. Correlating CNs and EMs, roof moss removal product.

EMs have correlations in performance with other EMs. For example, water consumption is positively correlated with pollution and toxicity (more water consumed leads to more pollution) but negatively correlates with biodegradable content (as water consumption increases, biodegradable content decreases).

Finally, as is shown in Figure 3.11, we develop targets for the product and illustrate, in this case, where the product sits compared to its competitors (basement of the house). To do this, the designers look at the factors with the strongest influence on customer needs, both functionally and environmentally, and develop appropriate engineering metric targets.

For example, if the two most important CNs are to remove moss completely, with little or no PPE required, the concentration and quantity of chemical, along with energy and water consumption, are important. Yet, as this needs to be accomplished with little or no PPE, biodegradable content must increase. Thus, the design team will set the biodegradable content at 50%, an increase over the 8% currently in use, and vastly more than the competition, whose product has no biodegradable content.

Figure 3.10. EM correlations, roof moss removal product.

Correlations	
Positive	+
Negative	–
No correlation	

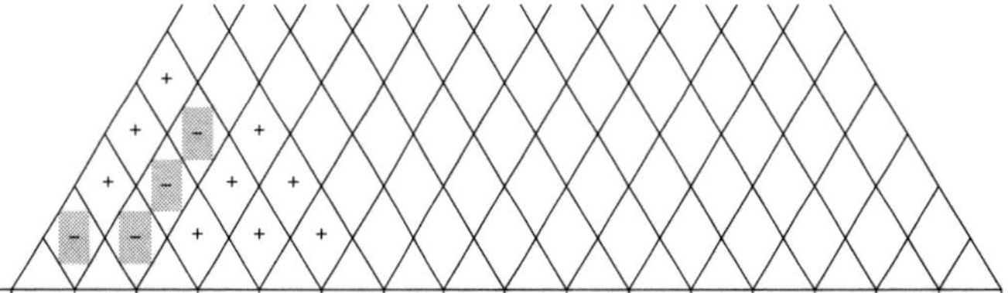

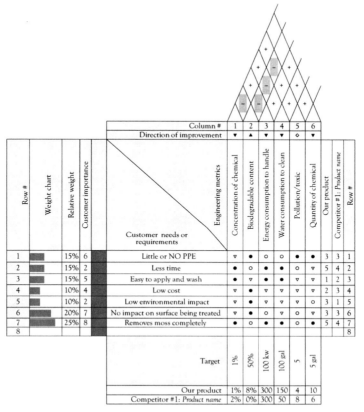

Figure 3.11. Analysis complete, with competitors evaluated.

Notice how the right-hand wall of the house can be used to show how competitors are achieving the CNs, again using data gathered via focus groups or surveys.

Workshop: QFDE

1. Consider a sustainable product of interest to you. Using a spreadsheet format, develop a list of customer and sustainable stakeholder needs for your product (CNs).
2. Develop a list of metrics that could be used to evaluate the sustainability of your product (EMs).

(Continued)

(*Continued*)

> 3. On the spreadsheet, show the relationship between your CNs and your EMs, using "+" to show that they are positively related and "-" to show that they are negatively related. Leave the box blank if their relationship is neutral.
> 4. Answer the following questions:
>   a. What makes developing targets for your product challenging?
>   b. Are there particularly difficult tradeoffs you need to make to improve one feature without sacrificing another?
>   c. If so, what kind of creative solution might you use to bridge these dual objectives?

Life Cycle Assessment

LCA can be used to assess the environmental or social effect of a product or process in a holistic way. It requires an evaluation of raw materials production, manufacturing, distribution, use, recyclability, and disposal activities in a product's entire life, along with all of the transportation required to support the product's existence. Typically, the goal of LCA is to create a starting point for process improvement, policy development, and other informed, product-related decisions. While environmental LCA is most popular, social LCAs have increasingly being used to assess the potential impact of a product or service on social issues. Additionally, *attributional* LCA considers the burdens associated with a product or process at a specific point in time, while *consequential* LCA focuses on the impact of a specific decision on a system, typically the long-term environmental and economic impacts of the decision. From a manufacturer's or retailer's perspective, LCAs are useful to quantify the amount of energy and raw materials used as inputs, as well as the solid, liquid, and gaseous waste generated at each stage of a product's life. Figure 3.12 shows the scope of LCA.

Example: Paper vs. Plastic Bags[7]

Whether or not stores should ban or charge for plastic bags is a popular debate in many cities, and the focus of government policy decisions in some municipalities. To help clarify the decision, LCAs have been done

Figure 3.12. LCA scope.

on paper and plastic bags, evaluating the energy required and pollutants created in each step of the bags' life cycles.

Looking at raw materials, paper bags are made from trees, a renewable resource, while most plastic bags are made from polyethylene, which is made from petroleum and is a nonrenewable resource. For manufacturing, paper bags begin with timber harvesting: the timber is pulped, made into paper, and then made into bags. Plastic bags, on the other hand, require petroleum or natural gas extraction, then ethylene manufacturing and polymerization, after which a bag can be created. Considering transportation, plastic bags weigh considerably less than paper bags, and take up less space in a truck and in a landfill. However, plastic bags can take five to ten years to decompose in a landfill, while paper bags take about a month to decompose outdoors; paper bags can, however, last considerably longer in a landfill depending on conditions.

In the final analysis, 100 plastic bags were calculated to consume 129,800 BTU of energy and generate 3.82 ounces of pollutants and solid waste. An equivalent carrying capacity of paper bags was calculated to consume 162,900 BTU of energy and generate 10.26 ounces of waste. However, more than 20% of paper bags are recycled, while only 1% of plastic bags are recycled. Additionally, plastic bags have been acknowledged to be very destructive to marine life habitats while paper bags disintegrate in water and have minimal impact on biodiversity. Thus, the environmental LCA alone does not conclusively answer the question of whether paper or plastic is better. However, it does give a manager or decision maker a strong basis of information for making a choice, depending on his or her priorities.

The Natural Step

The Natural Step (TNS) is a nonprofit organization founded by Karl-Henrik Robèrt in 1989, based on a set of irrefutable scientific principles from physics and natural law. This framework has been adopted by many international businesses to integrate environmental principles into their strategy and product design process. The four TNS system conditions state that to be become sustainable as a society, we must

1. Eliminate our contribution to the progressive buildup of substances extracted from the earth's crust (for example, heavy metals and fossil fuels).
2. Eliminate our contribution to the progressive buildup of chemicals and compounds created by society (for example, dioxins, PCBs, and DDT).
3. Eliminate our contribution to the progressive physical degradation and destruction of nature and natural processes (for example, over-harvesting of forests or the paving over of critical wildlife habitat).
4. Eliminate our contribution to conditions that undermine people's capacity to meet their basic human needs (for example, unsafe working conditions or not enough pay to live on).[8]

These conditions create a framework for assessing progress toward sustainable products and processes. For example, when looking at components and materials in a product design, or when examining stages of a manufacturing process, design teams can consider how the material or stage conforms to each of the system conditions, and then can adjust in "natural steps" toward a more sustainable direction.

Example: Max Hamburger Restaurants and TNS[9]

Most fast food chains are not highly regarded for the health attributes of their food, working conditions, and greenhouse gas emissions. But Max Hamburger Restaurants, Sweden's oldest and most popular burger chain, is changing perceptions. In 2007, Max partnered with TNS to move its supply chain in a more sustainable direction, applying TNS's framework to help define the company's options and improve its operations.

Working toward TNS's first condition (avoiding the concentration of substances extracted from the earth's crust), Max switched to 100% wind energy power, removed all toys requiring batteries from kids' meals, and transitioned to low carbon-emitting company vehicles. Working toward condition two (reducing concentrations of substances produced by society), Max stopped buying GMO food products, started converting all of its used cooking oil into biodiesel, and began recycling as much material it consumed and produced as possible, including food waste. For the third step (reduction of degradation by physical means), Max began to purchase all of its fish from Marine Stewardship Council-certified producers, purchase most of its paper products from Forestry Stewardship Council-certified producers, and invest in reforestation through Plan Vivo-certified projects in Africa. And finally, for the fourth step (not subjecting people to conditions that systematically undermine their capacity to meet their needs), the company stopped using trans fats, reformulated all of its product lines to be the healthiest in the industry, hired at least one staff member with a mental disability at more than half of its restaurants, and modified its leadership program to include sustainability issues.

Max's work on greenhouse gas reduction was particularly notable. The company calculated the climate impact of its menu, from farmer to guest, and realized that its beef products accounted for almost 70% of the chain's total greenhouse gas emissions. Max's menus are therefore now labeled so that guests can choose more climate-friendly food items, and all of the company's beef comes from Sweden, reducing its footprint. Additionally, Max reduced the beef content of its burgers by 18%. The labeling effort alone has led to a 15% increase in consumption of lower carbon products, like chicken fingers and vegetarian chili, and a great reduction in greenhouse gas emissions.

Max's leadership training addresses the science of sustainability as well as the company's efforts toward sustainability. The course is oriented toward managers, but cashiers can take a four-hour version of the class, resulting in top-to-bottom knowledge and buy-in. Max's sustainability efforts have increased employee retention and pride in work. In addition, customer loyalty increased by 27% between 2007 and 2009, while profits have increased by 500% since 2003. The company has received numerous sustainability-related awards and now has Sweden's most satisfied fast food customers, beating out the multinational chains in nationwide surveys.

Industrial Ecology and Cradle to Cradle Design

Industrial ecology views business as a series of material and energy flows, in which the material and energy outputs of one process can become the inputs for another. In this framework, industry is restructured to be self-regulating and self-renewing, creating a closed loop cycle. Ideally, complete recycling of materials in an industrial system is achieved, as it is in a natural ecosystem. In an industrial ecology framework, product creators (i.e., manufacturers) become responsible for product reuse, reconditioning, product life extension, and waste disposal, rather than users. Therefore, cyclical thinking dominates product and process design, versus linear thinking.

Building on industrial ecology concepts, William McDonough and Michael Bruangart developed a design philosophy called **Cradle to Cradle** (C2C), which was outlined in their 2002 book and later became a product certification system for products designed with their principles.[10] As shown in Figure 3.13, C2C design uses the premise of biological metabolism as a model for a technical "metabolic" flow of industrial materials. For product design, component parts are designed for continuous recovery and reutilization as "nutrients."

The C2C framework also posits the following ideas:

1. Eliminate the concept of waste, as "waste equals food." In other words, design products and materials with life cycles that are safe for human health and the environment and that can be perpetually

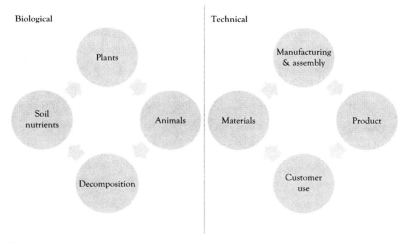

Figure 3.13. C2C philosophy.

reused through biological and technical metabolism. Additionally, create and participate in systems that can collect and recover the value of these materials after their use.

2. Power with renewable energy, or, "use current solar income." In other words, maximize the use of renewable energy in production processes.

3. Respect human and natural systems and "celebrate diversity." For example, maximize water quality, promote healthy ecosystems, respect local impacts, and guide operations and stakeholder relationships using a social responsible mindset.[11]

A number of companies have worked with C2C principles in product development and product certification, including Pendleton Woolen Mills (wool fabric), Method (baby lotion and other skin care products), Shaw Industries (carpet materials), Aveda (hair products), Herman Miller (chairs and office furnishings), and other construction, fabric, consumer, and furnishing companies. The case below illustrates C2C in action at Herman Miller.

Example: C2C at Herman Miller[12]

In the late 1990s, Herman Miller's advisory team researched various environmental design protocols to move their office furniture company in a more environmentally sustainable direction. After considering their options, they chose the C2C protocol, as it seemed to fit with the company's design and innovation culture. One of the first projects the team took on was the Mirra chair, a mid-level office chair, which would be designed from beginning to end with the C2C protocol. In order to operationalize this effort, the company's engineers, supply chain managers, manufacturing associates, and design consultants all had to adjust their processes.

The company broke the product development effort into several phases: (a) exploration, or, brainstorming the concept and creating high-level specifications; (b) development, which entailed dividing the product into modules with different teams assigned to each module, each of which would be evaluated with a score for appropriate material chemistry, disassembly, recyclability, and recycled content; (c) manufacturing, that is, designing the assembly process for the chair; (d) supply chain management, including getting suppliers on board with C2C concepts and appropriate materials, working with suppliers to assess materials, and updating the company's materials database; (e) sales and marketing, or, working with William McDonough (the C2C concept developer) to help promote the chair as the first design using the C2C protocol from start to finish; and (f) closing the loop, or developing a system for getting used chairs back to Herman Miller for recycling.

As could be guessed, challenges emerged during product development. First, the development team was successful in finding nontoxic and recyclable materials for most of the chair, but the arm pads were problematic. Making up 10% of the material cost of the chair, the standard PVC used in the pads met customer expectations for durability and cost, and the material was easy to shape during manufacturing. However, toxins were released when the arms were shaped. Another material with better environmental and health impacts, thermoplastic urethane, showed the same durability characteristics but was twice the price of PVC.

Each design alternative was given a DfE assessment based on the aggregated material chemistry, disassembly, recyclability, and recycled content scores for all component modules, and a final scorecard with a threshold score required for product acceptance. Interestingly, replacing PVC did not affect the chair's DfE score significantly as the contribution per part was based on weight. Regardless, on C2C's material and chemical list of "red" (known or suspected toxins), "orange" (unknown risk), "yellow" (low to moderate risk), and "green" (little or no risk), PVC was a "red," and thus was prohibited from use.

Another issue was figuring out how to close the loop. Getting the chair back to Herman Miller for recycling required a reverse supply chain. To achieve this, the company could either collect the discarded chairs from users itself, or it could use a third party to collect chairs. Alternatively, Herman Miller could ask retailers to collect chairs and develop their own process for handling used goods, or wait for community recycling efforts to catch up to DfE protocols. These choices had varying consequences with regard to corporate operations and costs. Ultimately, the company decided to rely on its dealer network to take back used chairs and repurpose them. However, Herman Miller believes that environmental regulations in many countries will eventually help create the reverse supply chain it desires, bringing the chairs all the way back for recycling.

Today, all new Herman Miller products are designed to the C2C standard, and many of the company's older products have been redesigned to meet the standard as well. The company today earns 55% of its sales from DfE-approved products, up from 51% in 2009.[13]

Biomimicry

The concept of **biomimicry** evolved from bionics, which is a science in which data about the functioning of biological systems is used to help solve engineering problems. In 1997, Janine Benyus published the book, *Biomimicry: Innovation Inspired by Nature,* and, according to her definition, biomimicry is a "new science that studies nature's models and then imitates or takes inspiration from these designs and processes to solve human problems." Benyus suggests looking to nature as a "model, measure, and mentor" for design, and emphasizes sustainability as an objective of biomimicry.[14] Biomimicry has gained widespread acceptance in the sustainable architecture community and in the sustainable building materials and textiles industries.

Examples of product development with biomimicry inspiration now proliferate beyond the well-known Velcro fabric closure example (mimicking a burr attaching to animal fur). For example, to create Lotusan®, an exterior coating, scientists studied how the wings of many large-winged insects, like butterflies, and many plant surfaces, remain dirt-free without any chemical detergents or energy expense. They found that in these instances, dirt was repelled due to the manner of interaction between surface topographies and water molecules. Using the micro-structural principles learned from this analysis, the product designers created a coating that can regain its cleanliness automatically after a rinse from a simple rain shower.[15]

Another example is Interface, a carpet producer, which used biomimicry principles for several floor treatment products, including TacTiles®, a carpet tile installation system. Inspired by examples of adhesion without glue in nature, such as sticky lizards' feet, the company designed tiles that could be installed without glue. Therefore, fewer volatile organic compounds are emitted. The lack of glue also means the carpet can be installed on hard surfaces without damaging the substrate, an additional product design feature.[16]

Conclusion

Sustainable product and process design is the first step in authentically incorporating social and environmental goals into a company's operations. It is also the last step, as products that are designed to be reusable or recyclable can help companies close the loop in supply chain management, or eliminate waste once a product has reached the end of its useful life. Sustainable product and process design extends from relatively easy and low-investment activities, like finding ecoefficiencies, to more complicated activities like quality function deployment for the environment, life cycle assessment, and cradle to cradle design. No matter the depth of effort or investment required, sustainable product and process design can have significant benefits for a firm, helping with cost cutting, branding, and marketing, and easier take-back of used products if demanded by consumers or regulation. The tools chosen for use by a firm will depend on its strategy and culture; however, knowing the content of this chapter is foundational for any company interested in the authentic pursuit of sustainability.

Checklist for the Practicing Professional

To assist with applying the ideas from this chapter, consider the following:

- Which products or processes in your firm likely need the most improvement?
- Who is responsible for those products or processes?
- What is your ultimate goal in revamping the products or processes?
- Who in your firm would be best at analyzing the products or processes under review?
- What framework might be most useful for revamping these products or processes?
- How might the design changes you make impact raw materials selection, supplier selection, purchasing methods, logistics, and product end-of-life management?

Recommended Readings and Videos

Readers interested in QFDE are referred to:

Abbie Griffin and John Hauser (1993). *The Voice of the Customer.* Marketing Science, Vol. 12, No. 1, pp. 1–27.

John Hauser and Don Clausing (1988). *The House of Quality.* Harvard Business Review, Vol. 66, No. 3, pp. 63–73.

Mansour Rahimi and Merrill Weidner (2002). *Integrating Design for the Environment (DfE) Impact Matrix into Quality Function Deployment (QFD) Process.* The Journal of Sustainable Product Design, Vol. 2, pp. 29–41.

CHAPTER 4

Sustainable Purchasing and Logistics

With globalization, companies are increasingly seeking the parts, products, and services they need from suppliers located worldwide. For example, China accounted for more than 20% of global manufacturing in 2010, with exports valued at $1.7 trillion.[1] Because most supply chains are now international in scope, supply chain managers often cope with cultural, language, and political differences, and face increased administrative and legal complexity. The lengthening of companies' supply chains also means that today, purchasing and logistics activities frequently have the greatest impact on the sustainability profile of a firm.

For example, Wal-Mart estimates that 90% of its greenhouse gas emissions come not from its own operations, but instead from the 120,000 companies that comprise its supply chain.[2] For companies that purchase and resell products and services, versus manufacturing or delivering services themselves, supply chain and consumer emissions can be as much as ten times their direct, or in-house, emissions. Moreover, longer supply chains complicate transparency. This means it is more difficult to ensure social integrity and responsibility in the supply chain, in addition to environmental practices. Thus, while many firms feel like they have a good grasp on their internal sustainability issues, monitoring and managing purchasing and logistics is equally critical.

In this chapter, we assess how a firm can move its supply chain in a more sustainable direction by making changes to its purchasing and logistics activities. We first address sustainable purchasing, explaining the concept of a supplier code of conduct. We then look at common certification programs, which help align suppliers with these codes of conduct. We examine the supplier selection process, and discuss the monitoring and auditing of suppliers. We conclude with a discussion of sustainable logistics, addressing ways to minimize resources and environmental impacts during the transportation process.

Sustainable Purchasing

In recent years, a best practices model for sustainable purchasing has emerged. This model, illustrated in Figure 4.1, has four stages of work. In the first stage, meaningful standards about supplier practices and behavior are developed. In the second stage, suppliers are selected and methods to measure and verify supplier practices and behavior are vetted. Third, implementation commences and compliance with the metrics established in stage two is monitored. Finally, the success of the supply chain is evaluated and the supply chain is improved, as needed. This final step is iterative in nature, focused on continuous improvement.[3] All of these steps are detailed below.

Step One: Develop Meaningful Expectations for Suppliers

Step one, the starting point for sustainable purchasing, focuses on deciding what is important to a firm and its stakeholders with regard

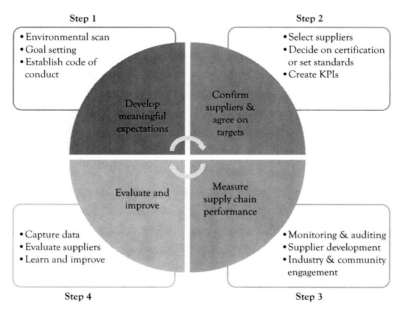

Figure 4.1. Best practices model for sustainable purchasing.

to sustainability. Many of the issues chosen will flow naturally from the firm's sustainability or corporate strategy. These issues will eventually evolve into a set of standards, or a code of conduct for suppliers.

Environmental standards may dominate a company's code of conduct if it uses sensitive resources or creates significant byproducts during manufacturing and supply chain processes. Likewise, socially responsible purchasing standards may dominate a procurer's code if labor issues are most salient; for example, production is dependent on labor in the developing world. For example, companies like Nike and Nestlé, who faced negative media attention and consumer backlash in the past about labor issues, have adopted codes that emphasize labor concerns. Nestlé's code of conduct for suppliers is shown in the side bar, for illustration purposes.

Nestlé Code of Supplier Conduct: Labour Standard

Prison and forced labour

The Supplier must under no circumstances use or in any other way benefit from forced or compulsory labour. Likewise, the use of labour under any form of indentured servitude is prohibited, as is the use of physical punishment, confinement, threats of violence or other forms of harassment or abuse as a method of discipline or control. The Supplier shall not utilize factories or production facilities that force work to be performed by unpaid or indentured labourers, nor shall the Supplier contract for the manufacture of products with subcontractors that engage in such practices or utilize such facilities. Where a Supplier is using labourers who are in an official prison rehabilitation scheme, such an arrangement is not considered a breach of the Code.

Child labour

The use of child labour by the Supplier is strictly prohibited. Child labour refers to work that is mentally, physically, socially, or morally dangerous or harmful for children, or improperly interferes with their schooling needs.

Working hours

The Supplier must ensure that its employees work in compliance with all applicable laws and mandatory industry standards pertaining to the number of hours and days worked. In the event of conflict between

(Continued)

(*Continued*)

a statute and a mandatory industry standard, the Supplier must comply with the one taking precedence under national law.

Compensation

The Supplier's employees must be provided with wages and benefits that comply with applicable laws and binding collective agreements, including those pertaining to overtime work and other premium pay arrangements.

Nondiscrimination

The Supplier shall not discriminate in hiring and employment practices on the grounds of criteria such as of race, colour, religion, sex, age, physical ability, national origin, or sexual orientation.

Freedom of association and collective bargaining

Unless prevented by governmental policies or norms, Suppliers should grant their employees the right to Freedom of Association and Collective Bargaining.

Source: Nestlé (2010).

To ascertain the most salient environmental and social concerns that should be present in a company's code of conduct, the company should assign an individual or team the task of answering the questions below. Note that these questions may also have been asked during recent strategic planning sessions that focused on sustainability; if so, the information gathered during that process may be of value in answering these questions.

- What are the relevant issues for our industry?
- Who are the experts on the different issues that could assist in standards development?
- Who are the suppliers that should be engaged in the process?
- What are the location-specific issues for our suppliers?
- What are the new issues cropping up for those suppliers?
- How relevant are those issues to our company?

Often, identifying sustainability concerns is not difficult to do, although crafting ways to authentically address those concerns may be complicated. For example, two recent explosions at Apple supplier factories in China have been widely reported in the media, and make clear that company's need to address issues related to worker safety; four workers were killed, and 77 were injured in these explosions due to inadequate ventilation of aluminum dust created during iPad polishing operations. While the explosions occurred at two different suppliers, one of these, Foxconn, had already been cited by critics as due to poor working conditions, in part because of recent worker suicides. In response to public criticism that Apple was inadequately addressing its most salient sustainability concerns—social issues—the company recently asked a third party reviewer, the Fair Labor Association, to audit several of its supplier factories in China. These audits are currently ongoing, however if significant issues are found and Apple takes a strong position on the problem, it could set a new social standard for the consumer electronics industry.[4]

As a company begins the process of identifying its most salient sustainability concerns, stakeholders should be engaged. Stakeholders can include consumer groups, NGOs, and current or potential suppliers who will eventually need to comply with the standards. If stakeholders are engaged from the beginning, they will tend to be more open to complying with any standards developed that are outside of their normal scope, rather than looking at these standards as obstacles. In addition, this multi-stakeholder method for developing standards creates an opportunity to address culturally sensitive issues, so that involved parties have a greater understanding of one another's perspectives; encourages the setting of reasonable targets, which further enhances buy in from affected parties; reduces barriers to implementation; and improves the overall sustainability of the supply chain.

Step Two: Confirm Suppliers and Agree on Targets

Step two is to connect suppliers with sustainability targets. Companies come at this task from different directions. A company may have an existing supplier base that they would like to have comply with their standards, or they may have an existing or developing standard for which they need to find or develop compliant suppliers. In either case, the buyer needs to collect information on the suppliers that are out there, do operational reviews to assess their current practices, prioritize measurements and metrics, and then categorize the suppliers. Potential suppliers could be at different stages of conformance. Some suppliers could be immediately ready to work with the sustainable purchasing standards; others could have poor sustainability performance but, with development and training, eventually reach conformance.

Some of the tools for supporting conformance are certification and key performance indicators. Additionally, the purchasing team should have an information system such as an **environmental management system** (EMS) to help gather and evaluate supplier data in relation to performance metrics. This system also needs to be able to disseminate performance data to suppliers in real time.[5] Other sustainable purchasing system requirements are summarized in Table 4.1.

As an extension of the conversation that began in the first stage of work, buyers and suppliers should meet during this second stage of work to discuss potential issues that could arise around the standard being developed by the buyer. Additional topics of discussion can and should include the use and selection of a certification program, the use and design of performance metrics, and the systems and processes with which performance data will be gathered. At this time, the buying team should ask the following questions:

- How can we ensure that we are not only selecting companies with established sustainability capabilities, but also supporting

Table 4.1. Sustainable Purchasing System Requirements

Supplier purchasing assessment
Objectives of sustainable purchasing program
Materials and classification of materials (recyclable, toxicity levels, produced locally, etc.)
Supplier base and key representative from each company

In-house purchasing assessment
Company's bargaining strength and strength of key suppliers
Company's strategic decision-making hierarchy for different purchased items
Organizational structure required to facilitate strategic development of suppliers
Company's process elements required to facilitate strategic development of suppliers
Company's behavioral elements required to facilitate strategic development of suppliers
Company's other available strategic tools required to facilitate strategic development of suppliers

Source: Author.

and developing those without established capabilities that have been good suppliers in the past?

- What mechanism will be used to raise awareness and increase communication with suppliers about sustainability targets? How will we offer suppliers the opportunity to resolve challenging issues regarding targets and processes?
- Which internal and external stakeholders should be a part of the assessment process used to ascertain the practicality of performance measures, and resolve issues?
- What type of supplier training may be necessary and who will provide this training?
- If certification is required, which suppliers are capable of meeting the certification standards and can afford the certification cost? Which suppliers need help meeting these costs, and how can our company help alleviate or subsidize those costs?
- If using a newly developed standard or guideline, have all the systems and processes needed to obtain reliable performance data and select suppliers been outlined?

Existing standards and certifications are one of the most important screening devices for supplier selection and development. Generally, these tools create institutionalized expectations between buyers and suppliers. Many of these standards articulate which key performance indicators and methods for measuring data are of most value, and outline an auditing process that can help identify which suppliers should be selected. Different standards, guidelines, and certifications are discussed next.

International Standards and Guidelines (Non-Industry Specific)

As mentioned previously, companies can create their own standards for suppliers or they can adopt an existing industry standard or certification program. Obviously, the latter eliminates the need to spend the time and energy creating a new standard or code of conduct. On the other hand, adopting existing standards can be challenging as these standards typically lack industry specificity and an auditing entity or body.

Some companies may opt for general industry certification, for example the **ISO 14000** family or the **ISO 26000** guidelines. The ISO 14000 program has been very popular in Japan, Germany, and the UK, with several thousand companies signing on. However, it has been slow to catch on in the United States. One of the reasons for this is that U.S. governing bodies haven't acknowledged the standard, whereas it has been incorporated into several national government standards in Europe, rendering it much more meaningful. Note that U.S. companies doing business in Europe may be required to adopt this certification scheme.

The ISO 14000 family covers environmental management systems, 14001 provides the EMS requirements, and 14004 gives the general EMS guidelines.[6] Overall, the requirements ask suppliers to implement a systematic approach to setting environmental objectives and targets; to identify and control the environmental impacts of their activities, products, and services; to demonstrate that targets have been achieved; and to improve their environmental performance continually. Other standards and guidelines in the family cover specific environmental aspects: labeling, performance evaluation, life cycle assessment, communication, and auditing.

In response to increasing consumer focus on social issues, the ISO 26000 guidelines have emerged.[7] The guidelines address seven core subjects of social responsibility: human rights, labor practices, environment, fair operating practices, consumer issues, and community involvement and development. For each subject, the issues are explained along with expectations and guidance for putting social responsibility into practice, along with voluntary initiatives and tools.

The highlights of ISO 14000 and 26000 are shown in Table 4.2.

Industry-Specific Standards and Certification

Depending on the industry, product-specific standards and certifications may be available to guide and implement sustainable purchasing programs. For example, a plethora of certification programs exist for agricultural products—from food and wood, to coffee and cotton. In addition to being industry-specific, these certifications can help shoppers identify aspects of a product or service that align with their values, but may not be readily transparent during the purchasing process.

Table 4.2. ISO Sustainability Series

ISO 14000 series
14001: EMS requirements
– Supplier should identify and control environmental impact
– Continually improve environmental performance
– Implement system to set environmental targets, achieve them, and demonstrate successes
14004: EMS guidelines
– Labeling, performance evaluation, life cycle analysis, communication, and auditing
ISO 26000 series
Social responsibility subjects
– Human rights
– Labor practices
– Environment
– Fair operating practices
– Consumer issues
– Community involvement and development guidelines
– Explanation of issues, how to apply principles into practice, best practices, voluntary initiatives, and tools

Source: ISO.

This, in turn, helps producers build consumer trust and capture the price premiums associated often associated with sustainability.

For example, one can easily detect color, size, and price attributes from observation; these characteristics are therefore referred to as **readily apparent attributes**. However, some content and process attributes are difficult for the purchaser to perceive through observation. For instance, one cannot detect the difference between genetically modified and conventional food items, or between organic, fair trade, or conventional cotton, through touch, taste, smell, or sight alone. These characteristics are therefore referred to as **credence attributes**, which refer to the content or physical properties of a product, or to its production process characteristics.

To capture the value associated with a credence attribute (e.g., the price premium on organic vs. conventional carrots), producers of credence attribute products must convey the existence of such attributes to purchasers in some way. To do this, the producer typically makes some kind of claim about the product, transmitted via labeling, a website, or another information source. One of three types of claims can be made: a **first**, a **second**, or a **third party claim**. The type of claim made can and will help purchasers determine the validity of the credence attribute.

First party claims. In a first party claim, suppliers state that they have produced their products a certain way. No outside verification applies. Rather, buyers need to simply trust the producer, or invest their time to assess the claim. Examples of first party claims are statements like "Made in the USA" or "eco-friendly." In the first case, the product could indeed be entirely manufactured in the United States. However, the product could also just be packaged in the United States, with no substantive manufacturing done there. In the second case, eco-friendly means nothing in particular, as this claim is not regulated or verified by any agency or organization. Therefore, although sustainability is implied, "eco-friendly" actually has no clear meaning or significance.

First party claims can also be issued by industry groups. For example, there are numerous industry groups claiming to handle animals in a humane manner. For beef, the National Cattlemen's Beef Association (NCBA) states that its herds are humanely raised, based on its guidelines for the care and handling of beef cattle. However, NCBA's guidelines specify that access to pasture is not required; that confinement to feedlots is acceptable; and hot iron branding, castration without anesthesia, and use of electric cattle prods are allowed. Additionally, NCBA does not audit its guidelines and the NCBA has declared publicly that it doesn't believe that auditing of animal care is necessary. Clearly, some consumers who are interested in animal welfare issues may disagree with NCBA's assertion that it handles animals in a humane manner; such are the risks of first party claims for consumers, however.

Second party claims. In a second party claim, a purchasing entity certifies that a producer has met a certain set of guidelines. The producer's assessment is performed by a person or organization that has a "user's perspective" interest in the product (e.g., traders, retailers, or consumers and their organizations). One of the challenges with this certification type is that collusion can occur between producers and sellers, at the expense of consumers. In short, both the producer and the seller may benefit from making certain claims; thus, the depth and significance of the claim may be less than what is implied.

Third party claims. In a third party claim, an independent party with no vested interest in the outcome conducts an audit to determine if a producer has met certain standards. Third party certifications are considered the most credible since the evaluating party is independent of the supplier, the retailer, and the consumer. Certifiers are public or private organizations responsible for accessing, evaluating, and verifying safety, quality, process, and other claims based on a set of standards and compliance methods. Examples of various third party certifications are shown, by industry, in Table 4.3.

Carbon Footprint Labeling, Standards, and Future Trends

In 2007, a small number of products sold in the UK offered carbon dioxide emissions labeling. Policymakers thought that labeling would create an impetus for producers to reduce the carbon footprint of their products, as the labels would allow shoppers to compare products' footprints directly. To date, many companies have attempted to calculate the footprint of their products. However, many have also found the process to be complex and costly—as much as $30,000 per product assessed. Additionally, different footprint estimation methods and country labeling standards make direct comparison challenging.

Over time, measurement techniques are becoming more standardized and today, a global standard is slowly emerging. Interestingly, while labeling was originally intended to support consumer decision making, many companies have found that the process of footprint assessment actually helps identify areas of supply chain waste, enabling reduced emissions. Today's labels also have more features, with information broken down to reflect emissions during manufacturing and during product use (highly influenced by consumer behavior). Information on a product's water footprint and potential impact on biodiversity is also often conveyed.

Different countries are moving forward with carbon labeling at different rates, and with different approaches. Japan, Korea, and Thailand have focused on product category rules for things like furniture, rice, consumer electronics, textiles, and chicken. The UK continues to advance its carbon standard, PAS 2030, which applies to many products and has influenced standards development in many other countries.

Table 4.3. Industry Third Party Certifications

Certification name	Industry	Certification details	Assessment measures
Rainforest Alliance	Forestry	Ensures that forests and farms are managed according to rigorous sustainability standards	Verification of standards
Energy Star	Electronics, appliances	Products earn label through high degree of energy efficiency; ensures customers lower energy costs and reduce pollutants	Government backed; assesses improvements to save energy costs
LEED	Building	Framework for identifying and implementing green building design, construction, operations, and maintenance solutions	A rating system; buildings earn points for their sustainability efforts and achieve ratings if they qualify
Responsible Jewelry Council	Jewelry	From mine to retail, the seal confirms ethical, responsible, and transparent social and environmental practices	Code; requires audits and verifications
Fair Trade	Mixed	Ensures workers are fairly compensated for their product; verifies agreed-upon environmental, social, and labor standards	Rigorous supply chain audits; high transparency and traceability are required
Better Cotton	Cotton	Standards for the cotton industry designed to phase out pesticide use, encourage careful water extraction, and protect drinking and other water from farm runoff	Voluntary program; data is collected, measured, and interpreted to evaluate success
Oregon Tilth	Agriculture	A full range of certification services that verify organic products; internationally recognized	Strict production standards, onsite inspections, and legally binding contracts
Marine Stewardship Council	Fishing	Requires that fisheries have sustainable fish stocks, minimize environmental impacts, and have effective management to respond to changes	Certified using a scientific methodology by an independent third party accredited certifier

Source: Author.

The UK's standard has been an impetus for two other global standards under development, which are expected to be complete in 2012 (ISO 14067 and the GHG Protocol). France, on the other hand, has seen significant activity from big retailers on grocery products. For example, customers at E. Leclerc stores can see how the footprint of the contents in their shopping cart compares with that of the average cart; footprint estimates exist for 20,000 products sold in the store. The French Standards Agency (AFNOR) is also going to be requiring labels that show footprint, usage, and other environmental data by 2012, encompassing products from food to apparel, along with wood and different types of furniture. These rules will also apply to imported goods, which will impact international suppliers.[8]

Companies that decide to carbon label their products face many challenges. Most notably, companies must work with their suppliers to determine and then reduce the footprint of their products. Often, suppliers are reluctant to reveal information about their processes, as they may need to disclose sensitive information that reveals true costs. In addition, consumer emissions can be a significant part of a carbon footprint; thus, consumers must be educated about ways to reduce their emissions. For example, washing a piece of clothing in cold water can significantly reduce the lifetime emissions of the product, as compared to warm or hot water washing. Another challenge is determining the cross-border emission calculation due to offshoring and outsourcing production. For example, the EU countries claimed that they reduced their total carbon emissions by 6% between 1990 and 2008, but this reduction was met by an increase in extra emissions associated with importing products from China. This shift resulted in an actual 6% increase in emissions for the period, overall.[9]

Key Performance Indicators

Most companies already use an array of **key performance indicators** (KPIs) to evaluate their suppliers, assessing topics related to finance (e.g., cost, return on investment, inventory, delivery cost); quality (e.g., number of stock-outs, lead time, lateness, customer satisfaction); time (e.g., cycle time, fulfillment time, traceability, response); and flexibility (e.g., volume or product). Should a company pursue a sustainability strategy, environmental and social KPIs will also be needed to evaluate sustainability performance. Many certification programs and standards spell out their measurement approaches and required KPIs, but sustainability standards developed in-house will require the creation of unique, "custom fit" KPIs. Even companies using an established standard or certification program may want or need additional KPIs to support their sustainability goals.

Environmental and social KPIs can be very industry- and standard-dependent. Environmental KPIs generally cover emissions, natural resource use, recycling and waste, while social KPIs cover labor topics, health and safety issues, community activities and investment, sensory impacts (e.g., noise, diet), and humane animal handling practices. Examples of sustainability KPIs are provided in Table 4.4. As should

Table 4.4. Environmental and Social KPIs

Category	Sample measures
Environmental KPIs	
Emissions	Carbon dioxide, methane, or other greenhouse gases per product produced (in kilograms or tons per unit)
Natural resources	Water, fuel, land, etc. per unit of product produced; energy or water per facility; food miles
Waste reduction/recycling	Waste, spillage, or leakage per unit; percent reclaimed or recycled material; percent reusable
Social KPIs	
Employees	Number of jobs created (local vs. offshore); percent full time vs. part time; number of employees trained; retention; absenteeism
Community	Money invested in community events; financial impact on local community; number supported and financial investment in charities
Health and safety	Percent insured workers; accidents per year; percent safety trained; number of toxic spills or leaks
Sensory impacts	Noise level; odor impacts; building vs. green space footprint; hours of operation; industrial zone usage
Humane animal practices	Number of downed animals; area of living space per animal; percentage of life spent outdoors; percent cage free

Source: Author.

be evident, each metric is accompanied by a standard that defines how the metric is measured. For example, a standard for percent absenteeism would use the total number of full time work hours in the category under review as the denominator, and the total number of absent work hours in the category under review as the numerator.

Step Three: Measure, Develop, and Manage Supplier Performance

As a company segues into the third step of the sustainable purchasing model—measuring supply chain performance—a few final tools need to be developed. First, a management system should be created to support supplier measurement and evaluation. Second, development programs should be created, to help suppliers better meet agreed upon sustainability targets.

A **supplier management system** needs to articulate specific, consistent methods for evaluating supplier progress toward sustainability targets. Thus, such a system must include the following: (a) a system of recording incidences of noncompliance, progress, and remediation, so that suppliers can be evaluated over time; (b) probationary periods during which noncompliant suppliers can develop plans and procedures to address issues; (c) a clear plan to deal with repeatedly noncompliant suppliers; and (d) a supplier recognition and rewards programs for suppliers who are compliant or those who make great progress at compliance, including praise and publicity for excellence when achieving sustainability goals.[10] Note that companies can employ local independent informants to gather intelligence on conditions at supplier plants, and suppliers' interactions with and impacts on their local communities.

With regard to supplier development, experts have defined development programs as any systematic organizational effort that creates and maintains a network of competent suppliers. At a macro level, this could mean continually seeking out new suppliers of sustainable materials. At a micro level, this means creating activities or programs that help existing suppliers continuously improve their quality, or waste or toxicity reduction efforts, such as information sharing and training.[11] Typically, a supplier development program will focus on a smaller supplier base of strategic importance. Thus, the program should address the following questions:

- How can the supplier base be incentivized to adopt the buyer's sustainability goals and commit to a long-term relationship with the buyer?
- What systems and tools should suppliers use to collect data and share information with the buyer?
- Which of the buyer's existing staff can be used to train suppliers? Who will develop the training materials, particularly for multilingual locations? Are there external trainers and firms that could support this effort?
- Is it feasible to offer a training conference for the supplier group, providing issue-based sessions, cross-supplier discussions, and knowledge sharing?
- Which companies should be in the development program? Can these suppliers be selected in a way that directs company resources and attention to the most critical suppliers?
- How can the buyer better support suppliers—for example, providing equipment, software, low interest rate loans for improvements, etc.?

Finally, it should be noted that at this stage of work, there is a great opportunity for buyers to further the stakeholder engagement process that, ideally, was launched when the sustainable purchasing model first began to be developed. In most situations, suppliers will not be in the same community as the buyer; rather, they will be in geographically distant places, nationally or internationally. While suppliers may have always had a good understanding of potential sustainability issues that existed in their communities, sharing this information with buyers can be challenging due to concerns over lost trust, contract losses, lack of understanding about cultural norms, and other issues. Thus, ongoing dialog as relationships and systems develop can help create incentive systems that actually work, featuring mindful and reasonable probationary and remediation periods, progress monitoring, and public awards and recognition for appropriate sustainability gains. Deep community and industry relationships can also help buyers identify new sustainability opportunities, and mitigate potential risks.

Step Four: Evaluate and Improve the System

The final step in the process of building a sustainable supply chain is for the purchasing company to have a periodic evaluation of the full supplier base and program. Most sustainability standards have a requirement for continuous improvement, thus the purchasing company does the analysis of the comprehensive supplier performance data (preferably quarterly). Using the KPIs, the purchaser can consolidate all of the supplier data into one report, with metrics and case studies that illustrate both high performers and compliance problems as learning examples. Having the report and supporting data audited by both in-house and external experts (NGOs, academics, and other concerned stakeholders) adds transparency and legitimacy to the process. Through the reporting system, an in-house sustainability task force can help efforts to improve sustainability performance in a continuous way.

Example: Truitt Brothers and Food Alliance[12]

Since 2005, Truitt Brothers, an Oregon manufacturer of canned bean and fruit products, has been working with Food Alliance, a third party certification program also headquartered in Oregon, to achieve its sustainability goals. This, in turn, has required significant work with the company's raw materials suppliers to ensure supply chain compliance.

For example, the company recently launched a canned chili product that it wished to have Food Alliance-certified. In order to achieve this certification, and have the Food Alliance logo featured on the can label, both the canning facility and the ingredients producers had to be Food Alliance-certified. Third party inspectors audited and toured suppliers' facilities and farms, using detailed evaluation criteria and KPIs that assessed the extent to which suppliers' operations met Truitt Brothers' and Food Alliance's desired management outcomes. Specifically, owners, managers, and key staff were interviewed by inspectors to understand the systems, practices, and decision making approaches used in growing and canning operations. Many criteria and tools were specific to the individual products in the chili (beans, tomatoes, beef, etc.), since the sustainability concerns associated with these products vary (e.g., bean farming has a vastly different environmental impact than cattle ranching).

In general, to become Food Alliance-certified, farmers and ranchers must meet minimum thresholds in four areas: pest and disease management, soil and water conservation, human resource management, and wildlife habitat conservation. Producers who do not pass the minimum threshold on any one criteria are given time to remedy the situation before the auditor returns to reevaluate the particular issue of concern. Once all the ingredients producers and processors pass the minimums, then the product is allowed to use Food Alliance's certification seal on the label.

Supplier Purchasing Scorecards and Assessments

Scorecards are internally generated tools that suppliers must fill out yearly in order to sell to a given buyer. Scorecards can assist with sustainable supply chain management in several ways. First, they can help streamline the supplying process, as suppliers know ahead of time the buyers' sustainability concerns and buying criteria. In essence, they can help create a "prequalified" list of suppliers. Scorecards can also help buyers become more creative about sustainability solutions in supply chain management, as noteworthy ideas often percolate up from suppliers during the reporting process. These ideas can then be shared with other suppliers, helping the sustainability of the supply chain overall. Lastly, scorecards can help build consumer trust, as the use of scorecards is an indicator that buyers are examining the tiers of their supply chain to assess sustainability performance, and not just focusing on internal issues, which are often very limited compared to true, "whole chain" impacts.

Proctor and Gamble (P&G) provides a good example of a scorecard in action.[13] In 2010, P&G launched its scorecard, focusing on 400 strategic suppliers. The card was developed after 18 months of collaboration with suppliers and other key stakeholders. The company hoped that most of its suppliers would fill out the scorecard and that it would become a consumer goods industry standard. After the first year, 300 scorecards had been submitted by suppliers and about 40% of the cards offered at least one innovative idea in the area of sustainability. This included a chemical supplier that has since begun work with P&G on renewable materials development. Rick Hughs, P&G's chief purchasing officer, explained the scorecard's immediate benefits:

> The scorecard is the right tool to give us that snapshot across our supply chain so we can identify where to focus our collective supply network sustainability efforts, develop ideas to work on together, and reward those who excel.[14]

Wal-Mart also uses an assessment tool to help evaluate its suppliers' sustainability activities and profiles. A comparison of the supplier evaluation tools used by P&G and Wal-Mart is provided in Table 4.5. Note that both systems have a weighting scheme for supplier answers, so that

Table 4.5. Supplier Scorecards – P&G and Wal-Mart

Proctor & Gamble purchasing scorecard	Wal-Mart supplier assessment
(Electric) Energy usage	Have you measured and taken steps to reduce your corporate greenhouse gas emissions?
(Fuel) Energy usage	Have you opted to report your greenhouse gas emissions to the Carbon Disclosure Project?
(Input/withdrawal) Water usage	What are your total annual greenhouse gas emissions reported in the most recent year measured?
(Output/discharge) Water usage	Have you set publicly available greenhouse gas reduction targets? If yes, what are those targets?
Hazardous waste disposal	If measured, please report the total amount of solid waste generated from the facilities that produce your product(s) for Wal-Mart for the most recent year measured.
Non hazardous waste disposal	Have you set publicly available solid waste reduction targets? If yes, what are those targets?

(Continued)

Table 4.5. Supplier Scorecards – P&G and Wal-Mart—(Continued)

Proctor & Gamble purchasing scorecard	Wal-Mart supplier assessment
Kyoto greenhouse gas emissions direct (scope 1)	If measured, please report total water use from facilities that produce your product(s) for Wal-Mart for the most recent year measured.
Kyoto greenhouse gas emissions indirect (scope 2)	Have you set publicly available water use reduction targets? If yes, what are those targets?
Annual output	Have you established publicly available sustainability purchasing guidelines for your direct suppliers that address issues such as environmental compliance, employment practices, and product/ingredient safety?
P&G sustainability ideas and initiatives supported (description)	Have you obtained third party certifications for any of the products that you sell to Wal-Mart?
Fines and sanctions ($ value)	Do you know the location of 100% of the facilities that produce your product(s)?
Environmental management system (yes, partial, no)	Before beginning a business relationship with a manufacturing facility, do you evaluate the quality of, and capacity for, production?
Data protocol (description)	Do you have a process for managing social compliance at the manufacturing level?
Optional Questions: Renewable energy Kyoto greenhouse gas emissions indirect (scope 3) Potential recycled, reused, recovered Transportation fuel efficiency, industry certifications	Do you work with your supply base to resolve issues found during social compliance evaluations and also document specific corrections and improvements?
	Do you invest in community development activities in the markets you source from and/or operate within?

Sources: Procter & Gamble (2009) and Wal-Mart (2011) Supplier Sustainability Assessment.

a summary score can be created. As P&G is a consumer goods manufacturer and Wal-Mart is a retailer, one would expect some differences in the design of their supplier assessments. Indeed, P&G's tool has a focus on resource inputs and outputs, with no questions on social sustainability. Wal-Mart's tool has social sustainability questions related to compliance and community development.

Workshop: Scorecard Design

1. Using P&G and Wal-Mart as examples (see company websites for more information, if needed), design a scorecard for your company's purchasing department. Use Excel.

    a. Be sure to indicate the core strategy of your company on the scorecard, and explain how sustainability connects to your core strategy.

    b. Include no more than 15 questions on the scorecard.

    c. Be sure to identify appropriate KPIs, and explain how suppliers should obtain/measure the data that informs these KPIs.

2. How will the questions be weighted and who will decide on the weights?

3. How much improvement should be expected each year?

Logistics: Beyond Cost Minimization

Although the goal in logistics management has traditionally been to minimize costs, inbound and outbound transportation decisions also critically impact the sustainability of a firm. Every logistics system involves the following physical elements: a vehicle (car, train, boat, aircraft, bike, etc.), an energy source (oil, natural gas, electricity via coal, wind, nuclear, solar, and human power, etc.), and infrastructure (roads, port, airport, etc.). However, logistics systems also include the individuals who support and implement the physical aspects of the system—that is, the people who dictate organizational structure and institutional makeup, and those who operate the physical system and are affected by it, as shown in Figure 4.2. Thus, decisions in all of these areas must be made carefully, as they impact both the cost and the sustainability considerations of a firm.

Organizational Context

The context that an organization works in sets the stage for its logistics decisions. Different locations offer different options to the decision maker. For example, in many parts of the United States, freight rail infrastructure

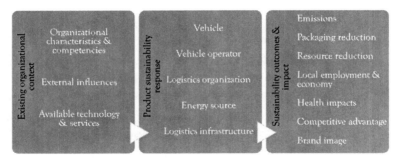

Figure 4.2. Sustainable logistics framework.

is limited and at capacity, either because new rail line development is not physically feasible, or because investments in rail transport have been limited relative to places like Europe and China. Therefore, in lieu of using heavy rail transport, which is very energy-efficient, sustainability improvements may need to focus on how to most efficiently and effectively use trucks. Decisions would then need to be made about engine selection, truck weight, optimal inbound and outbound loading strategies, load sharing, and so forth.

Similarly, political and economic issues deeply influence trade dynamics—such as tariffs or subsidies for certain products. Depending on the importing country, quotas on things like textiles may force logistics staff to choose more expensive and less sustainable options for shipping, in order to get materials into a country before a given quota is reached.

The strategy and core competencies of the company will also shape logistics decisions. For example, if a company is pursuing a cost leadership strategy, then the logistics department will make decisions that support cost minimization. This results in companies like Wal-Mart setting energy use reduction goals for logistics activities that, in effect, support both cost reduction and environmental priorities, as eco-efficiencies during transport are prioritized. However, in this example, while sustainability has at least one clear "win" (energy reduction), social sustainability goals, like buying products from regional or local producers, may end up being secondary, if such products cannot be efficiently transported to centralized distribution centers by producers.

Finally, the technologies and services available in a given location or company will influence the choices available to logistics decision-makers.

For example, a company may not have sophisticated route planning or load combining software. This will then limit its ability to minimize miles traveled, emissions, and costs. Similarly, many produce companies have thought about distributing fruit and vegetables in returnable plastic totes, to reduce packaging waste. However, the lack of large scale, regional tote washing facilities required to meet the sanitation needs of the industry limits achievement of this aspiration for many.

Product Sustainability Response

As a company's operating context shifts, logistics practices need to be assessed to ensure they optimize and align with current conditions, goals, and strategies. As industry interest in sustainability is increasing, a substantial context shift is indeed occurring for some companies—that is, those that have prioritized sustainability as a goal or strategy. Sustainability considerations for vehicle selection, vehicle operation, the logistics organization, the selection of an energy source, and logistics infrastructure are detailed below.

Vehicle choice affects delivery costs, delivery frequency/flexibility, and environmental impact. Boat transport is the cheapest and most environmentally friendly logistics option. However, water transport is not available in all instances due to geographical constraints. Additionally, shipping by boat is very time-consuming, although this constraint has been alleviated to some extent by the construction of more modern ports. Rail is also an affordable and energy efficient transport option, but time can be a factor due to a lack of capacity in rail yards. Regional rail lines have also been eliminated in some areas, requiring intermodal truck transport to connect hubs with main lines. Trucking has gained in popularity in recent decades as it allows for flexible routing and frequent deliveries, and is relatively inexpensive. However, trucks tend to rank poorly with regard to environmental impact. Therefore, truck transport is not always desirable. Air freight is the fastest shipping option available to manufacturers. However, it is also the most expensive and energy consuming option. Bikes can be used for local deliveries in many urban environments, with great flexibility and superior delivery time over trucks in some high traffic areas.

With regard to vehicle operators, companies need to determine the skills and technologies that operators need to improve sustainability performance. Considerations include ensuring operators know about a firm's sustainability goals; supporting operators with techniques, trainings, and decision-making tools that enhance environmental performance; creating or enhancing processes that help operators relay findings and ideas about environmental performance back to the firm; and rewarding good performance. An example of an activity that can improve environmental performance at the operator level is reducing truck idling, which wastes an enormous amount of fuel. In lieu of idling, truckers can instead plug in their vehicles for winter heat and electricity at designated plug-in areas near truck stops. This solution also applies to operators of other types of delivery vehicles. Delivery vehicles can also be supported by global positioning system (GPS) systems that assist with location finding, and routing software that optimizes delivery routes and reduces mileage, which clearly supports environmental goals.

The resources and abilities of the logistics department also need to align with sustainability goals. These people are the ones executing the sustainability strategy and they need appropriate training, the ability to gather performance metrics for various shipments, and supportive technology. For example, to improve transportation efficiency and environmental performance, production and shipping planners' ability to consolidate material flows depends on available scheduling techniques, intermodal transport, and fleet management systems. Similarly, sustainably minded organizations should consider how other functional areas might impact logistics. For example, redesigning packaging and using packaging optimization processes can help lighten shipping loads and increase the number of items shipped per container, thus reducing per unit shipping costs and environmental impacts. Operations managers can use process optimization with the goal of minimizing lead times and reducing resource use in production and warehousing, thus improving opportunities for consolidation.

The energy source used to support warehousing and logistics activities has a significant impact on the environmental footprint of an organization. Typically, the vehicle chosen for distribution limits choices with regard to energy use. For example, electric power and biodiesel can be used with lightweight small trucks, but are not suitable for larger and heavier vehicles. Warehouses in sunny locations are good candidates for solar electric panels, which can often supply all of a building's energy needs.

Finally, logistics infrastructure can be improved—or different infrastructure-related decisions can be made—that will improve the sustainability performance of a firm. For example, companies can use full mixed load trucks to move products to regional or urban warehouses, where they are then broken down for local distribution by small light load trucks or bikes.

Sustainable Logistics Outcomes

As the goal of the sustainable logistics framework is to improve the sustainability performance of the logistics system, tracking measures need to be in place to monitor the system's performance. For example, IKEA has a strategic goal of using its warehouse and transportation resources efficiently. However, one of the major contributors to warehouse and transportation inefficiency is packaging, which IKEA uses a lot of. Thus, while products need to be protected by packaging, the air and materials in IKEA's packaging must be minimized if the efficiency of the company's transport load units and vehicles is to be maximized. Therefore, each product group at IKEA continually looks for ways to package their products more efficiently. A tracking system then measures things like units packed per container, weight per pallet, transport energy use, emissions per item, and breakage per units shipped. The goal, of course, is to maximize efficiency, which helps IKEA achieve cost and environmental goals.

Companies can also use "delivery in full and on time" (DIFOT) measures to gauge their achievement of logistics goals and service performance. In order to improve on this measure, companies can build inventory, and then use different types of vehicles and technologies to support load mixing and full vehicle loading. Different tactics will impact cost and environmental and social measures; thus, it is important to have comprehensive measures that reflect all aspects of sustainability.

Example: Organically Grown Company's Sustainable Logistics Strategy

Started by farmers with health-conscious motives, the Organically Grown Company (OGC) distributes certified organic produce throughout

Oregon and Washington. Although the company first distributed produce grown only at its own farms—small- and mid-sized, family-owned enterprises—the company has grown considerably since its founding in 1982, and today distributes organic produce and vegetables from all over the world.

Building from a sustainability-focused mission, which creates a strong organizational context for green innovation, OGC has developed an environmentally friendly distribution strategy, illustrated in Figure 4.3. The company tailors its logistics activities to accommodate the needs of both long distance travel and inner city delivery, and chooses its delivery vehicles, routes, and technologies to maximize environmental performance. For example, OGC uses hybrid-electric trucks and biodiesel fuel as part of its Green Fleet Initiative, which helps with environmental performance on the road. The company also uses bicycles for inner city delivery, which enhances last mile environmental performance.

The truck that OGC chose for long distance delivery is the Kenworth T300 hybrid-electric heavy duty truck (although electric truck technology is now more diverse, this was one of the only alternative fuel trucks available at the time OGC made its purchasing decision). In contrast to standard semi-truck fuel performance, which averages around 9 MPG, OGC's hybrid truck achieves about 14 MPG, making it ideal for long distance transport. To help reduce dependence on foreign fuel, 27.5% of OGC's fleet uses biodiesel B99, a blend of recycled vegetable cooking oil.

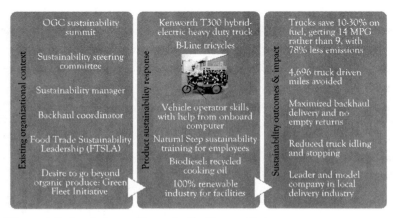

Figure 4.3. Logistics at Organically Grown Company.

Though this fuel costs more than standard fuel, the decision to pay a premium was made to support the company's values and mission. Recently, OGC also figured out how to reduce diesel consumption by using electric standby to power refrigeration units while its trailers are docked.

Vehicle drivers participate in ongoing training to increase the efficiency of OGC's trucking operations. On-board computers record exactly how each vehicle is operated, producing feedback about drivers' speeds and stop frequencies. Each driver can examine their reports and then work to reduce idling and speeding, which consume excess fuel. Miles per gallon (MPG) and case per gallon metrics are also studied to identify areas of improvement. Every detail of delivery vehicles is examined to help identify how efficiencies can be increased—for example, drag reduction due to wider tires. One problem OGC is currently facing is that its trucks are returning empty, which wastes both fuel and money. To help address this, OGC recently hired a backhaul coordinator to help maximize backhauls. This has helped keep OGC's trucks full; freight volume increased in 43% in 2010, and average fleet MPG performance also improved.

For urban Portland, OGC decided to have its products delivered via the B-Line, a company that uses motor-assisted, cargo-equipped tricycles to deliver products in dense areas. B-Line enables more economical and timely delivery than large truck delivery, because of constraints on vehicular speed and parking in the urban core. OGC was B-Line's first partner, and the bike company has since grown significantly, reducing truck congestion in downtown Portland. Interestingly, B-Line faced a similar issue to OGC in that after delivery, its cargo bikes would return empty. The company solved this problem by partnering with the Oregon Food Bank, bringing back nonperishable items after deliveries.

OGC measures its environmental impact using the Food Trade Sustainability Leadership (FTSLA) guidelines, and a formula developed internally to derive greenhouse gas emissions from diesel fuel bills. According to these metrics, OGC's environmentally focused strategies have had positive sustainability impacts. The company's hybrid trucks use 10–30% less fuel than a conventional truck, and the use of the 99% biodiesel blend produces exhaust with 78% fewer CO_2 emissions than petroleum diesel. Thus, 27% of OGC's vehicles qualify as "Clean Air" vehicles under the Federal Diesel Emissions Reductions Act. Using B-Line for last mile delivery has also resulted in 4,696 fewer truck miles driven. Remarkably, because of these efforts, OGC is managing to drive down its emissions, despite robust corporate growth.

Conclusion

Purchasing and logistics activities play one of the most significant roles in improving the sustainability of a firm. From the attributes of raw materials to the shipping methods for getting the final product to customers, these decisions affect multiple sustainability measures. In this chapter, we have provided tools for creating sustainable purchasing and logistics practices such as codes of conduct, certification programs, supplier selection and training, and finally auditing and monitoring systems for suppliers. While many companies may have headed down this path as suppliers to Wal-Mart or other major businesses with sustainable supply chain improvement programs, others may have the opportunity to positively influence their own supply chains. It is an area ripe with opportunity for business leadership and differentiation.

Checklist for the Practicing Professional

Does the Sustainable Purchasing Department have a:

- Policy Statement: This would communicate buyer goals and sustainability strategy.
- Supplier Code of Conduct: This would align with the policy and address how business will be done with suppliers, standards, and penalties for nonconformance.
- Minimum Performance Standards: Those are relevant to sustainability metrics and could comprise a certification requirement.
- Individual Product Specifications: Other product-relevant criteria.
- List of additives, materials, or chemicals to avoid.
- Preapproved Materials: Products that can quickly move through purchasing decisions.

- Request for Proposal: These can include sustainability and product specifications along with details of the purchaser's long term sustainability program.
- Surveys or Audits: Similar to Wal-Mart or P&G's purchasing audits.

Supplier Selection Criteria (Ranking): Details how suppliers are ranked and selected from a competitive set.

- Preapproved Supplier list: Those suppliers that have met all criteria.
- Auditing Procedure: This would detail the frequency of audits by purchasing department to supplier (yearly, etc.).
- Supplier Performance Reviews: Typically would occur after auditing and financial year end.
- Programs for Buyer–Supplier Collaboration: Ways to improve performance metrics that involve participation from both parties.
- Supplier Training Program: Complete process for initial and ongoing training with suppliers.
- New Product Development: Process for integrating suppliers into new product development cycle.
- Sustainable Logistics Strategy: A complete process for managing and monitoring the impact of the logistics decisions and a plan for continuous improvement.

CHAPTER 5

Sustainable Product End-of-Life Management

At one time, consumer products had very long lives, with repairable and reusable parts and minimal or reusable packaging. However, in the 1920s, the concept of planned obsolescence emerged, coinciding with the move toward mass production and cost minimization. With this approach, product designers and manufacturers intentionally create products that have diminished durability and need quick replacement—the goal being to make consumers buy updated products sooner. As a result, we now see products like furniture, which historically lasted a lifetime or through multiple generations of users, now last just a few years. For example, it is not uncommon for college students to fit their rooms with IKEA furniture and toss it in the dumpster when school is done, as it is too unstable to withstand heavy duty transportation. New furniture then needs to be bought for the student's next place, or their next phase of life.

Product packaging has followed a similar path. When steel cans were introduced in 1953 for soft drinks and beers, the beverage industry quickly moved away from returnable and reusable bottles in favor of the cans. With no container deposit or return system, these cans rapidly increased municipalities' solid waste volumes and the amount of litter on the side of highways. Eventually, solid waste tonnage grew faster than population growth, as more manufacturers realized the marketing potential of the packaging and switched to disposables. As landfills reach capacity, new capacity must be sought, and as new landfills are often located far away from populations, the waste transportation costs of municipalities increase. As a result, many governments today employ strategies to manage costs and litter. Most charge hefty fees for waste, particularly for bulky products or those with toxic content, and some state governments require deposit fees on glass and plastic bottles to encourage their return and recycling.

In response to these issues and trends, a new idea is emerging: product end-of-life management. In this approach, manufacturers are choosing to take responsibility for their products' entire life cycle, which can be challenging, but also beneficial from an environmental, social, and economic perspective, particularly when regulation exists or is on the horizon. In this chapter, we examine these and other reasons a business might consider "closing the loop" on its products—or, reducing the impact of products that have completed their useful life by reclaiming, reusing, and recycling them. We also discuss methods to reduce the use and impact of packaging.

Reasons for Closing the Loop

After years of improving the cost and efficiency of **forward supply chains**, many businesses are now looking to create **reverse supply chains**. Rogers and Tibben-Lembke define the reverse supply chain as "the process of planning, implementing, and controlling the efficient, cost-effective flow of raw materials, in-process inventory, and finished goods from the point of consumption back to the point of origin for the purpose of recapturing value or proper disposal."[1] This can also be thought of as "closing the loop," or product end-of-life management (EOL).

Companies that engage in reverse logistics have estimated that it accounts for approximately 4% of their total logistics costs.[2] While some see this as a burden, especially if the take-back is required by legislation, others see a closed loop supply chain as an opportunity for competitive advantage. As shown in Figure 5.1, a closed loop supply chain—which has both forward and reverse flows—offers a company many opportunities for innovation and value creation. For example, recycling and reselling used materials in secondary markets can generate additional revenue while reducing disposal fees, and reclaiming used parts for use in "new" manufacturing activities can reduce costs. These and other benefits are described in more detail below.

Environment and Economics

From an environmental and economic perspective, using the landfill as an EOL solution is problematic. In an increasingly resource-constrained

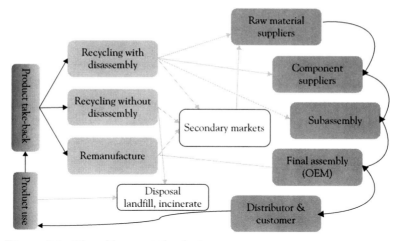

Figure 5.1. Closed loop supply chain.

world, land and raw materials are both becoming more scarce, and increasing in value. Thus, to bury materials underground is illogical, particularly if they are toxic, or have innate value. In landfills, toxic materials often leach into groundwater and contaminate freshwater systems, to the detriment of living things, in addition to taking up space that could be utilized for other productive activities. In landfills, potentially valuable materials are also made inaccessible, necessitating additional effort for industry to find new, even scarcer materials, versus reusing what was already on hand.

Some businesses see environmental stewardship as a priority, and have leveraged this value in a way that has helped them achieve a competitive advantage over others. For example, Herman Miller, Inc. chose to be proactive and design office furniture without toxic materials, and to craft products that could be disassembled and recycled. This has helped the company build its brand as one of the world's leading furniture makers. In contrast, other companies end up being reactive with their EOL strategies, as fines and legislative activities make landfill use either costly or prohibited. Most experts agree that landfill costs are going to continue to rise and environmental regulations covering the disposal of toxic and other items are going to continue to increase. Even in locations that do not require manufacturers to take back their products, the product may not be allowed in the landfill, creating a conundrum for users that may eventually force producers' hands.

Branding

Companies like Nike, and other apparel manufacturers, are often criticized for the short life cycle of their fashion products, which in turn creates waste and clogs landfills. To counter this negative image, several have instigated product take-back programs that give used clothing to the needy and build positive press for the company. For example, Hanna Anderson, the children's clothing company, requests that customers send back their worn products and offers participants a discount on the purchase of new clothing in return. The "Hannadowns" are then distributed to shelters, schools, and other charities. Similarly, Nike asks customers to bring their used shoes back to their retail stores to be shipped back to Nike. The company then shreds the shoes to create athletic surfaces like basketball courts and running tracks; it donates the material to build the courts and gives organizations the money needed to maintain them. These prominent displays of corporate social responsibility contribute to these companies' positive brand image, while incentivizing more thoughtful consumer purchasing.

Consumer Expectations

In the United States, and in many other countries, consumers expect to be able to return products if they are unsatisfied. Additionally, many companies make products that are good for only one season; older styles and inventory must be moved out to make way for newer goods, as newer goods demand better prices and have better margins. While the "old" products may not be at their actual end-of-life, having cost effective ways to manage this flow of goods is imperative. Thus, supply chain managers have devised ways to get products back from retailers in an efficient and effective way and dispose of them in a manner that maximizes their remaining value. Outlet stores, eBay, and other secondary markets are examples of ways to support the revenue maximizing effort. In short, some reverse supply chains already exist as a response to customer demand, inventory management, and revenue needs.

Legislative Activity

In the United States, the idea of **extended product responsibility** (EPR) has been slow to gain acceptance. However, certain industry groups have taken the lead in dealing with their toxic waste stream from used products. For example, Hewlett-Packard, Nortel, Frigidaire, and Xerox have adopted EPR, and industry-wide programs have been created to recycle nickel-cadmium batteries and auto bumpers.[3] Because of the slow response from business, state legislators are also adopting laws to deal with problem waste streams, either through required collection systems or fees covering the cost of product disposal, also known as **advanced disposal fees** (ADFs). Today, more than 15 states have laws requiring retailers to take back vehicle batteries, 22 states enforce ADFs for tires, and some have fees on motor oil and large household appliances. Other states have focused on particular product-related environmental issues, like toxic waste from household chemicals, paints, and batteries.

The European Union (EU) has taken a more aggressive stance toward product disposal legislation, particularly as it applies to waste electrical and electronic equipment (WEEE), due to these products' typically toxic content. Under the EU's WEEE directive, the first priority is the prevention of waste electrical and electronic equipment, followed by reuse, recycling, and other forms of waste recovery to reduce disposal needs. It also seeks to improve the environmental performance of all operators involved in the life cycle of electrical and electronic equipment—such as producers, distributors, consumers, and operators directly involved in the treatment of WEEE.[4]

Under the mandate, member states are required to create and maintain a database of producers, indicating the quantities and categories of equipment sold and collected through reuse, recycling, and recovery activities within the EU. Exported waste is also tracked, by weight or by quantity. This data is then transmitted to the commission on a biannual basis. A final requirement is that the WEEE symbol be placed on products that fall under one of the ten product categories illustrated in Table 5.1. All products from these categories manufactured after 2005 must be taken back by producers, and tracked as part of the responsible waste disposal effort.

Other countries have followed suit in their EOL programs. Japan has mandatory take-back of many similar product categories, while individual U.S. states such as California have passed laws making manufacturers, retailers, and consumers responsible for recycling and the responsible disposal of

Table 5.1. WEEE Product Categories

Category	Examples
Large household appliances	Stoves, refrigerators, washing machines, heating and cooling devices
Small household appliances	Vacuum cleaners, toasters, clocks
IT and telecommunications equipment	Computers, printers, phones
Consumer equipment	Radios, televisions, video cameras
Lighting equipment	Lamps and bulbs
Electrical and electronic tools	Drills, saws, machine shop tools, sewing machines
Toys, leisure and sports equipment	Video games, slot machines, electric vehicle sets
Medical devices	Cardiology, dialysis equipment
Monitoring and control instruments	Smoke detectors, heating regulators
Automatic dispensers	Dispensers for beverages, solid products, money

Source: Waste Electrical and Electronic Equipment (2003).

electronic products.[5] As this type of legislation continues to expand to other countries and U.S. states, it is reasonable to expect that soon, all EEE producers will be impacted by this legislation, regardless of where their products are sold. In particular, any company that is likely to sell in the EU will need to be compliant, as the EU prohibits these devices from being sold in EU countries if they do not comply with WEEE mandates. EEE producers must therefore consider how their products' designs and supply chains will affect their ability to be compliant, and begin tackling the processes and costs associated with item recovery, reuse, and recycling.

In conclusion, companies can be either proactive or reactive when deciding to close the loop in their supply chain, and being proactive can lead to a competitive advantage for companies that consider waste reduction an opportunity rather than a liability. However, implementing a take-back program can be challenging, drawing on all of a company's strengths with regard to product and process design, logistics, and continuous improvement. The following section lays out a recommended approach for evaluating the fit of the closed loop concept with your company's current supply chain setup, and suggestions on how to transition your operations to better accommodate closed loop supply chain management.

Product Take-Back and Recycling

As mentioned, product take-back can be a source of competitive advantage for some companies, as a closed-loop supply chain can have better environmental, social, and economic performance than a forward supply chain in some instances. However, this is not universally true for all products and companies at this point in time. Currently, the relative benefits and costs of a take-back program depend on several important factors, including the inherent reusability and recyclability of used products, the ease with which they can be repurposed or recycled, and the existence and depth of secondary markets for parts or packaging that cannot be repurposed. There are also strategic issues to consider regarding who will manage EOL activities.

These factors have environmental, social, and economic consequences. From an environmental perspective, bringing products back can add transportation effort, and processing used materials can in some instances increase energy or chemically intensive processing needs. From a social perspective, such efforts also pose potential safety threats. Finally, from an economic point of view, extra transportation and processing adds costs. Likewise, the value of reclaimed parts may be too low, and the depth and breadth of secondary markets too lacking, to make recycling or repurposing used products economically viable.

These dilemmas can be solved, however. Environmental and social challenges can frequently be addressed through product and process redesigns that allow a product to overcome constraints; note that these efforts may require significant investment in research and development or process technology to create a viable closed loop. The economic dilemma can be remedied by investor interest, customer demand, government legislation, and subsidies. Figure 5.2 illustrates a closed loop evaluation tool for firms to use when analyzing and comparing different product recovery strategies.[6] The steps in this tool are discussed next.

Step One: Develop Metrics and Collect Data

The first step in evaluating the potential of a closed looped supply chain is to evaluate existing sustainability performance data—or to determine baseline performance. Evaluation criteria and scorecard data from

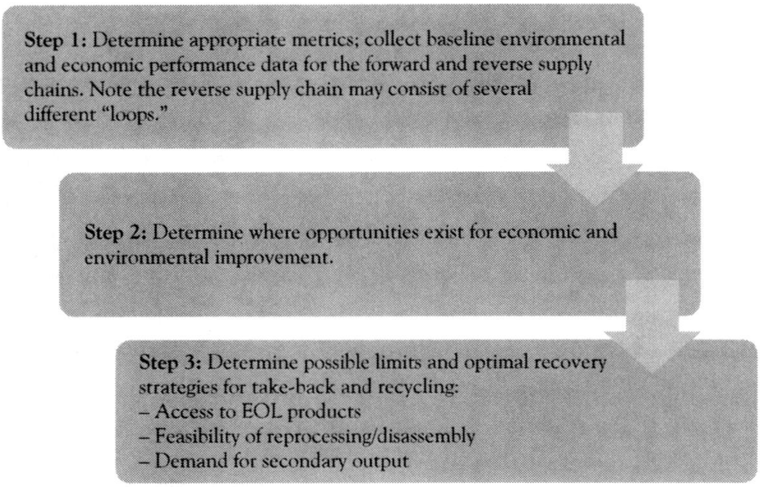

Step 1: Determine appropriate metrics; collect baseline environmental and economic performance data for the forward and reverse supply chains. Note the reverse supply chain may consist of several different "loops."

Step 2: Determine where opportunities exist for economic and environmental improvement.

Step 3: Determine possible limits and optimal recovery strategies for take-back and recycling:
– Access to EOL products
– Feasibility of reprocessing/disassembly
– Demand for secondary output

Figure 5.2. Closed loop evaluation tool.

previous chapters can support this need. Depending on the industry, the Life Cycle Inventory database can also provide useful information about the environmental performance of major processes; please see the end of this chapter for a link to the database.[7]

For example, looking at a typical cotton shirt, environmental impacts stem from four main activities: production (growing cotton, spinning and weaving, dyeing and finishing); transportation (truck transportation from an offshore factory to port, boat to the United States, U.S. rail to distribution warehouse, and truck to retail shops); customer use (washing, drying, and ironing); and finally, end-of-life processing (reuse, recycling, composting, and incinerating). In the forward supply chain, the primary environmental impacts typically occur when products are transported to retail outlets, and during the use phase. For example, washing shirts in hot instead of warm or cold water can double consumer energy use.

For the apparel's reverse supply chain, the environmental impact depends on the quality and fiber content of the item. While some used clothing may end up in the landfill, clothing may be resold to other consumers on Internet auction sites or through thrift and consignment stores, or donated to charity. Because the supply of clothing at these outlets overwhelms the demand, about 80% of charitable donation clothing is resold to textile recyclers. These businesses sort clothing by item, size, and fiber content. Valuable clothing goes on to consignment shops or collectors' markets around the world, or is bundled for bulk sale in developing countries. The remaining clothing, about half, continues on to a second life as a "new" product. That is, it is chemically or mechanically recycled into raw material for use in other apparel or non-apparel products.

For example, Trans-America Trading Company, one of the biggest of the roughly 3,000 textile recyclers worldwide, processes more than 12 million pounds of postconsumer textiles per year. The product not selected to go on for a second life as apparel is turned into absorbent rags for industrial use or recycled into fiber for use as upholstery stuffing, insulation, paper products, etc. Researchers estimate that reusing 1 ton of polyester and cotton clothing requires only 1.8% and 2.6% of the energy required to manufacture these goods from virgin materials, respectively.[8]

Thus, continuing with the example, a clothing producer would need to determine the cost of each process and an estimate of the environmental and social impacts incurred during the processes that comprise their forward and reverse supply chains, in order to establish a baseline regarding sustainability performance. The company would then be positioned to start thinking about what it could do to improve the environmental, social, and economic performance of its supply chain—for example, educating consumers about product usage and washing, developing in-house take-back and recycling programs, creating an in-house product repair program, etc. Additionally, a company should start thinking about the kind of infrastructure and services required to execute its closed loop concept—such as free return shipping, retail outlet collection points, and so on. An example of a company that has crafted a reverse supply chain for its clothing is Patagonia.

Example: Patagonia's Common Threads Initiative[9]

For the 2011 holiday season, Patagonia initiated its Common Threads Initiative for apparel. In its marketing campaign, the company asked consumers to sign the following pledge:

> I'd like to become a partner in the Common Threads Initiative
> to reduce excess consumption and give the planet's vital systems
> a rest from pollution, resource depletion and greenhouse gases.

Patagonia agrees to build useful things that last, to repair what breaks, and recycle what comes to the end of its useful life. I agree to buy only what I need (and will last), repair what breaks, reuse (share) what I no longer need, and recycle everything else.

The company's website provides tips on reducing apparel consumption (buy things that last, launder less to extend life, and don't buy unless needed); repairing existing products (through the company or through local tailors); reusing products (sell or pass on used products); and recycling (send used products back to the company for use in new fibers or fabric). The company supports these four concepts with product designs focused on durability and the use of recycled fabrics, and a reverse supply chain that gets products back from customers and into appropriate channels, as shown in Table 5.2.

Step Two: Assess Opportunities for Improvement

The next step in evaluating the potential of a closed loop supply chain is to find opportunities for performance improvement in the reverse supply

Table 5.2. Patagonia's Reverse Supply Chain

	Consumer marketing message	Patagonia company activity
Reduce	Don't buy what you don't need Use care guide to clean and maintain products for long term use	Design products to last a long time and be useful Develop care guide for maintaining and extending life of all products
Repair	Send products to Patagonia for repair Use local tailors	Policy of 10-day turnaround for repairs Design for easy repair Fair price for repair
Reuse	Donate clothing to charity, or sell used clothing through company's Common threads eBay site	Develop company reuse site and eBay site Donate factory seconds to activists and disaster relief
Recycle	Return used Patagonia clothing back to the company via retail locations or mail Keep all clothing out of landfills	Develop new fibers out of recycled fleece Take back 45 tons of material and make 35 tons of new clothing from it

Source: Author.

chain. In the recycling and reuse area, there are two dominant options: **recycling without**, or **recycling with disassembly**.

Recycling Without Disassembly

Products like apparel, tires, plastic, glass, and some metals are typically not disassembled after they are used; rather, some combination of grinding and sorting is employed to break them down for reuse. The products are either sorted initially, or after an initial grind step, which breaks down materials through shredding, shattering, or compression. For example, glass bottles often go to a glass factory when they are recycled. At the factory, they are sorted by color and then shattered into small pieces, where they are mixed with new material, melted, and formed into new bottles. In contrast, CRT monitors—which were popular before flat screen technology overtook the market—go to a special recycler with a crusher that then is capable of separating out different materials from the monitors. Recycling without disassembly is typically best for companies that sell a wide range of products or have limited flexibility in changing their products' designs. Additionally, there are often external companies that specialize in this service, like the textile recycler mentioned above.[10]

If a company chooses to go this route and has responsibility for the recycling process activity, there are things to consider that can affect the company's sustainability performance. Certain grind and sort activities can create toxic emissions, particularly in the electronics world, and therefore processes must be designed to contain toxins and prevent exposure; protective systems will add cost to the process. However, even with this constraint, self-recycling can be a good scenario if the company can use the recycled materials in its own "new" products and save on raw materials—the technical practicality of this, as well as the economic benefit, clearly needs to be analyzed before proceeding, however. More often, material cannot be reused by the company and is sold to a secondary component or materials salvage market, and any material that cannot be sold on that market ends up in a disposal stream. Thus, while a company may not have the ability to significantly change a product to enhance its reusability and economic value, it should strongly consider what kinds of small changes could have a large impact on parts recovery and value—for example, choosing slightly different materials, the type and placement of fasteners, changes to adhesives or welds, and so on.

Recycling With Disassembly

As legislation increasingly calls for EOL programs for large consumer goods and electronics, companies are increasingly being required to disassemble their products to recover value, reduce landfill contribution, and protect the environment from the toxic subassemblies. While some may see this as a burden, others have found huge opportunities for innovation and value creation by actually designing their new products with disassembly, recycling, and reuse in mind, also known as **Design for Disassembly** (DfD).

Decisions made during the design phase have a significant impact on the environmental performance of products. Studies found that as much as 85% of the life cycle costs[11] and 50% of the product costs[12] result from design phase decisions, while up to 70% of costs[13] are affected by manufacturing process decisions. On the process side, DfD benefits include ease of assembly, maintenance, reparability, and upgradability; all of these improvements reduce the cost and time of assembly and service. Economically, the improved designs offer higher recovery rates for parts and lower landfill costs since more materials go back into the primary or secondary materials markets than the disposal stream. DfD concepts can have multiple benefits for sustainability performance, as well, as highlighted in Table 5.3. In short, the recycling with disassembly approach adds process steps but has potentially more sustainability and economic performance benefits than the recycling without disassembly approach.

As an example, BMW designed the Z1 Roadster with plastic side panels that come apart like the halves of a walnut shell. Originally, glue or solder was used in the bumper assembly. By replacing these with fasteners, bumpers come apart more easily and the materials can be recycled. Today, the portion of BMW's cars that can be recycled is 80% by weight, and the company is aiming for 95% recyclability. The automobile industry in general is starting to excel at designing products for easy disassembly and remanufacturing; many automobile parts are now recycled into the "rebuilt" market, from full engines to water pumps and carburetors.

Table 5.3. Design for Disassembly Rules

Approach	Benefit
Don't mix materials	Sorting is easier; fewer suppliers
Focus on fasteners Minimize by integrating parts Use 1 fastener to hold together many parts Screws are faster than nuts/bolts	Easier assembly; easier maintenance; less time consumed assembling and disassembling
Avoid glue unless water-soluble or heat-reversible	Higher recovery rates; less contamination
Minimize different components	Lower sorting time; less material to waste stream
Improve visibility of high value or toxic parts (label)	More downstream value received from batteries, circuit boards, etc.
Include disassembly instructions	Easier to reclaim value and avoid landfill
Create fit with the larger system	Easier to get parts back or into the right channels

Source: Waste Electrical and Electronic Equipment (2003).

The steel frames go to scrap processors, where the demand is high and continues to increase.

Step Three: Decide on a Strategy

The final step in evaluating the potential of a closed loop supply chain is to determine the best strategy for take-back and recycling activities given the constraints in a company's system. First, a company assesses limitations on its access to EOL products. Next, the company determines the feasibility of reprocessing or disassembly, and limitations on those processes. Finally, a company evaluates the market demand for recycled or reused components and considers how that demand may shift with legislation, marketing, and improved quality of used components.

Many cities and municipalities have recycling infrastructure that handles glass, paper, aluminum, and other waste streams. But products that do not fall into the categories handled by a municipality lack a built-in take-back system, requiring a company to create a closed loop system itself via other relationships. For example, when Herman Miller developed its first DfD office chair, the Mirra, a furniture take-back supply chain did not exist in the United States. The options for getting used chairs back were to ask customers to bring their chairs back to a Herman Miller dealer-retailer; to create an alternative take-back channel, like shipping direct; or to use a third party supply chain business. Obviously, there are costs and benefits to each of these choices. The company opted for the first option, but this created an added burden on retailers for proper disposal of the chairs when they were returned.[14]

There are other examples of companies that have worked out methods for EOL recovery. Hewlett-Packard (HP) started a program to take back its ink and toner printer cartridges. The consumer has the option of using postage paid labels or envelopes to send the cartridge directly back to the factory, or they can use a big box retailer like Staples as a drop-off point. Staples offers an in-store coupon to encourage product return, and now takes printer cartridges from most of the major printer manufacturers, which helps create economies of scale for the process.[15]

Another successful example of product take-back is the Kodak single-use camera. Starting in 1990, Kodak developed a relationship with photofinishing outlets to return used cameras to Kodak's sorting centers. Kodak pays a fee to outlets for the returned cameras (both their own and other manufacturers'). At the sorting center, competitors' cameras are sent to their factories through an exchange agreement, and the Kodak cameras are either recycled or sent to Kodak's Guadalajara, Mexico factory for reuse in "new" disposable cameras. Internal parts that are still functioning are reused, and the plastic housing is ground and recycled. Today, the recycling rate for the cameras is 84%, the highest recycling rate for any U.S. product.[16]

In short, in analyzing its access to EOL products, a company needs to evaluate the cost and potential channel disruption from using an existing recycling system; its forward supply chain relationships; the potential for reverse activities, with incentives for participation; and potential workarounds or third party options if existing infrastructure or relationships will not suffice.

Next, a business should determine the feasibility of reprocessing or disassembly and ascertain the limitations on those processes. For example, some products, like construction steel, can be recaptured through deconstruction practices rather than demolition. However, time constraints, manual labor costs, and increased safety hazards can make deconstruction too costly relative to demolition, with regard to the benefits of selling the recovered structural steel. Thus, a 100% reuse rate on steel is difficult to achieve, as most contactors will only reclaim steel sections that are relatively easy to access via demolition, and of a high quality.[17]

Note that during this phase of work, it may be best to evaluate recycling approaches, recovery rates, the potential for resale, and the potential for revenue generation using existing channels and product designs to frame analysis. As a longer term strategy, then, businesses should continually assess how product and process changes could improve disassembly and value recovery.

Finally, a company should evaluate the market demand for recycled or reused components, and consider how the market may change with legislation, marketing, and improved quality of used components. For example, Figure 5.3 illustrates the difference in **life cycle cost** (LCC) and energy requirements for three different types of steel products: primary, recycled, and reused steel (used fabricated parts such as sections). Here the reused steel has the lowest energy requirements and LCC costs. However, market demand is a limiting factor for reused steel; without incentives for cost savings, most builders will choose new steel parts due to convenience and perceptions of lower risk.[18] And, sustainably oriented builders only choose reused steel if it is cost neutral with primary or recycled steel. The current pricing for reused steel therefore does not create an incentive for the building industry to go to the extra effort to carefully recover steel sections for reuse.

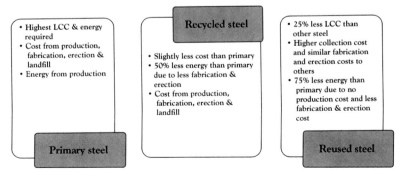

Figure 5.3. Life cycle cost and energy requirements for different steel products.

In conclusion, in most industries, recycling without disassembly has lower recovery rates due to contamination from mixed materials, limited choices for material resale, less revenue generation, and limited technical and new product development knowledge. Proactive businesses will therefore look for opportunities to integrate DfD into their new product and process development so as to encourage and enable recycling with disassembly.

Reverse Supply Chain Participation

Most businesses will look for a low-cost option for their reverse supply chain activities, especially when facing third party intervention, like government legislation. Often, third party recyclers and reverse logistics suppliers are called on to support take-back activities. However, a business may also work with members of its existing supply chain, like retailers. If this route is pursued, however, beware of new issues created due to a reorientation of power in the supply chain, stemming from a new interdependence created by the take-back directive.

If the firm decides to completely outsource recycling, it will typically choose the quickest and lowest investment solution with minimal channel conflict. The downside of this option is that the firm forgoes any opportunities to gain knowledge about potential DfD ideas and value creation. Additionally, it might lose control over designs and materials; thus, the relationship with the outsource company requires specific protective contracting and oversight. As the firm's participation in the reverse supply chain increases, closed loop supply chains become more viable, recycling processes may provide an opportunity to sell the service to others, scarce materials access is improved due to a reclaiming of used parts, and higher levels of learning and material recovery are obtained.[19]

In contrast, making retailers an integral part of a take-back program alters the traditional relationship between the buyer and seller. Without cooperation and commitment from retailers, many of the companies practicing EOL take-back activities would not be able achieve a sustainable competitive advantage. In the disposable camera example, Kodak pays a fixed fee and transportation cost per camera to its retail collectors and is now dependent on the retailer to fulfill this role if it is to have a stable supply of parts for new cameras. It is important that producers recognize the power shift and create relationship-building incentives, and employ other non-coercive strategies, to maintain and improve sustainable supply chain performance.

Packaging

Clearly, improving the disassembly and reusability of products is essential if a company has enhanced environmental performance as a goal. However, reducing the environmental burden of packaging is no less important an undertaking; of the 181 million tons of solid waste taken to municipal landfills in the United States in 2008, container and packaging waste made up 42%—or close to 76.76 million tons—of waste, swamping other categories, as shown in Table 5.4.[20] While the bulk of glass and aluminum waste was generated by beer and soft drink containers (3.7 million tons), paper and paperboard packaging makes up a whopping 38 million tons of waste annually. Bulk shipping and consumer packaging waste are primary contributors to this problem; thus this area is ripe for improvement.

Table 5.4. U.S. Municipal Waste Stream Generated from Products (2008)

Category	Thousand tons
Nondurable goods (newspapers, books, plastic utensils, disposable diapers, etc.)	58,710
Durable goods (tires, appliances, furniture, carpets, etc.)	45,670
Paper and paperboard packaging	38,280
Plastics packaging	13,010
Wood packaging	10,670
Glass packaging	10,050
Steel packaging	2,550
Aluminum packaging	1,880
Other miscellaneous packaging	310

Sources: Franklin Associates, a Division of ERG.

Bulk Packaging

Bulk packaging is used in a firm's supply chain for transportation and storage, and the category covers everything from pallets, drums, and boxes to gaylords (corrugated bulk shipping boxes). When Henry Ford first created the Model T assembly line, he requested suppliers use a specified wooden box to ship their parts to Ford. When the boxes of parts came to the plant, the wood from the box was used to make the floorboards of the cars. Any leftover wood was used for another startup business, Kingsford Charcoal.[21] Today, companies have similar reasons to conceptualize their bulk packaging as valuable, specifically the high cost of bulk packaging and the high cost of waste generation and disposal.

Ideally, reusable bulk packaging can alleviate transportation waste problems; however, this kind of packaging requires an efficient takeback system of its own to ensure investments in such packaging are not lost. Moreover, such packaging may be somewhat custom, as container designs need to fit the needs of the user. Obviously, companies that control their internal supply chain have an easier time of implementing reusable packaging programs; however, such companies must also examine the costs and benefits of their traditional packaging and transportation methods relative to the costs of purchasing, retrieving, and cleaning reusable packaging.

That being said, such investments can be extremely worthwhile. For example, Johnson & Johnson began using reusable gaylords for interplant shipping, domestically and internationally, and achieved a three-to six-month payback on its container purchasing costs. Similarly, John Deere & Co. had a two-year payback on its reusable crate program, used for shipping between retail outlets. Table 5.5 illustrates key success factors in reusable container programs.

It is estimated that there are almost 2 billion pallets in use in the United States every day. To support this demand, yearly production of pallets is close to 814 million, consisting of 500 million new wood, 300 million recycled or reclaimed wood, and 8 million plastic pallets. The remaining 6 million pallets are made of metal or paperboard.[22] Pallets are becoming a significant waste issue, as more than a third of U.S. landfills no longer accept them and others charge additional fees for their disposal. Additionally, wood pallets require many board feet of new wood from

Table 5.5. Reusable Container Success Factors

Success factor	Outcomes
Shorter transportation distances	Lower overall program cost, lower transportation cost, fewer containers required
Frequent deliveries	Fewer containers to accumulate, less space required, less damage and losses to container
Fewer parties involved	Easier to track containers, less opportunity for loss, easier to manage
Number of container sizes	More sizes = better cube utilization and lower transportation cost; Fewer sizes = less variety to purchase and manage, less storage cost
Partner buy-in	Partners may incur significant costs and work and must be compensated accordingly

Sources: Rodgers, D. and R. Tibben-Lembke (1998). Going Backwards: Reverse Logistics Trends and Practices. Reverse Logistics Executive Council.

forests, particularly hardwoods. Plastic pallets and containers are slowly gaining acceptance and have numerous advantages related to safety, cleanliness, longevity, product protection, and uniformity. However, the upfront cost of one plastic pallet can be $40 to $150, depending on its durability, while a comparatively sized new wood pallet is about $7 to $15.

Container pools can help companies overcome some of the costs and problems associated with reusable packaging retrieval, particularly in situations where supply chain partners are located in geographically dispersed areas, making retrieval costly. In a container pool, the pool company purchases millions of containers or pallets and leases them to companies for a fee—typically a charge each day a container is used. Obviously, this situation would not work well for companies that need to store their products on pallets for a long time; rather, such arrangements are useful for companies that simply use pallets to meet their product transportation needs.

The idea of the reusable container is not completely modern. Figure 5.4 shows the cycle of one well-known reusable container type: the beer keg. Using this example, we can illustrate the costs associated with reusable containers.

Clean kegs are filled in the brewery and picked up by a distributor. The distributor takes the filled kegs to its warehouse for storage. When orders arrive from pubs and restaurants, the distributor takes its trucks, with multiple products onboard, to these establishments, and replaces the empty kegs with the full ones. The empties are taken back to the

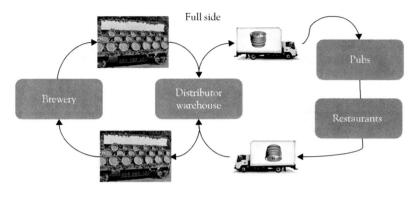

Figure 5.4. Reusable container example: Beer kegs.

distributor's warehouse and sorted by brewery (kegs have the brewery's label on them because there are typically only a few keg styles available). The next time the distributor goes to the brewery for a pickup, they return the empty kegs. The brewery then cleans and repairs any damaged kegs and refills them for the next delivery.

The costs to the brewery of this system includes buying kegs (upwards of $150 each), and if the brewery has X taps to cover, the brewery needs at least 2× kegs to cover the distribution cycle. In addition, kegs will need to be bought to cover growth in demand, pipeline inventory, and keg loss, with roughly 4–6% as the industry standard keg loss rate.[23] The brewery must also cover the cost of keg inventory management, cleaning, inspection, repair, modification, fill, and storage. On the distribution side, there is a transportation cost for the forward and the reverse side of the chain. The distributor also has costs related to inventory management and storage of both full and empty kegs. If the brewery requires national distribution, kegs can end up with a large geographical spread, as well.

All returnable packaging faces similar cost issues. Obviously, those companies that are already set up with an integrated forward and reverse flow can accommodate returnable packaging most readily. For example, regional wineries have realized that they too can use a keg approach for house wines sold in local restaurants, a recent trend in the western United States and in Europe. However, companies that have a heavy forward flow emphasis, like apparel retailers, which typically use third party shipping services like

USPS, UPS, or FedEx, cannot easily accommodate returnable packaging and thus must rethink their entire closed loop.

Consumer Packaging

As shown in Table 5.4, consumer packaging—particularly food and beverage containers—is another significant part of the waste stream. Because most people consume food items at least three times a day, food packaging is a major contributor to municipal waste and makes up 50% of all packaging sales, by weight.

Consumer packaging has become an important part of a firm's marketing and branding effort. In addition to conveying brand and marketing information, packaging must protect the product during transport and while on shelves. Food packaging in particular has to address unique issues like preservation, portability, and stackability. In a recent Nielsen study, researchers determined that consumers were willing to give up some things like storability, convenience, and portability for more environmentally friendly packaging attributes. However, they were less willing to give up protective features that keep products hygienically safe and in good condition.[24] Understanding these requirements will help innovative companies come up with more sustainable packaging solutions. For example, the beverage industry used 46% less packaging in 2006 than in 1990, even with a 24% increase in beverage sales during that time.[25]

Other consumer product companies are evaluating their packaging and aggressively working to reduce waste and costs. For example, Wal-Mart is working to reduce packaging in its supply chain by 5% by 2013. To support this effort, Wal-Mart has adopted several purchasing strategies and tactics. For example, the company recently created a consumer electronics packaging design challenge for its suppliers. Accepting the challenge, HP designed a way to sell its notebook PC in a recycled laptop bag, which uses 97% less packaging than a typical laptop. Exclusive to Wal-Mart, the notebooks come in a 100% recycled fabric carrying bag with a couple of protective plastic bags. The company can fit three notebooks in each shipping box, also dramatically reducing space and packaging requirements. According to Scott Erickson, HP's environmental program manager for its consumer PC business, the company can now get 31%

more products on each pallet. The packaging that remains contains no foam, and has only one piece of paperboard with product information.[26]

Example: Dell Computer Packaging

Dell has been working on reducing its packaging, setting a goal in 2008 of being the industry leader in computer packaging sustainability by 2012. Over this four-year period, Dell estimates it could save $8 million and eliminate 10,000 tons of packaging material if it achieves its goals. Dell's strategy uses a 3C approach, which focuses on the "cube," the "content" and the "curb." Specifically:

- Cube—How big is the box? Can it be smaller?
- Content—What is the packaging made of? Can it be made of something better?
- Curb—Is it easily recycled?

On the cube side, Dell has already shrunk its packaging volume by 11.7%, exceeding its initial 10% goal. In addition, if a customer orders several items, products can be bundled together in a multipack, which further reduces packaging. On the content side, 33% of Dell's packaging material is recycled, which is approaching the company's goal of 40%. All the business client product boxes are also made of 100% recycled corrugated cardboard, and considerable research has gone into creating recycled cushioning materials, like 100% recycled thermal-form HDPE and air cushions. Another new packaging product for minicomputers and netbooks is made from renewable and compostable bamboo. On the curb side, 68% of the material used in Dell's packaging can be recycled curb-side, close to the company's goal of 75%.[27]

Conclusion

Many companies find product-specific environmental improvements challenging, particularly the application of DfD concepts to products, technologies, and processes that change rapidly. But by considering a product's end-of-life experience during the design phase of work, the ease and profitability of a reverse supply chain can be greatly enhanced. Packaging reduction is also an area where many companies can find opportunities for improvement. Thus, managers from any industry should be able to incorporate at least some of these concepts, and reduce their reliance on the landfill. Innovative managers may also be able to turn product end-of-life management into a competitive advantage.

Checklist for the Practicing Professional

When considering product design and end-of-life management, consider the following:

- Is it easy to disassemble the current product? How many steps are required and how could they be reduced? What is the level of difficulty that exists? Are special tools required?
- How are parts are fastened together? How could this be improved or simplified?
- How many different materials are used in the product? How could this number be reduced?
- Are valuable or toxic components easy to identify in the product during disassembly?
- What does the company's packaging supply chain currently look like?
- Can packaging be reduced and still achieve essential objectives?
- What would a returnable packaging chain look like, and what are the current barriers to implementing reusable packaging?
- What are the potential costs and benefits of a reusable packaging chain?

Recommended Readings and Videos

- National Renewable Energy Laboratory. *U.S. Life Cycle Inventory Database* (http://www.nrel.gov/lci/). The LCI database was developed to assist LCA practitioners in determining products' environmental impacts, and provides substantial information on products' energy and material flows.

- Wal-Mart. *Sustainability 2.0 – Packaging* (http://walmart-stores.com/Video/?id=1229). Readers interested in packaging reduction may want to view this fascinating video from Wal-Mart, explaining the relationship between product design, packaging design, logistics, cost savings, and sustainability.

CHAPTER 6

Emerging Trends

Whether companies are required by consumers, retail partners, or regulators to adopt more sustainable supply chain practices, or are choosing on their own to initiate sustainable practices, the playing field for supply chain management is clearly changing. Just as the quality and lean movements of the 1980s and 1990s transformed the way businesses were managed, sustainability concepts are today taking root, with no reversal of the trend in sight. Rather, continuous adoption appears to be the norm, as businesses realize that the resources that sustain their operations are becoming limited, that instability created by environmental and social problems can pose a severe supply chain threat, and that consumers want to see industry and individual businesses do better.

For example, in one recent CEO survey, respondents indicated that a scarcity of natural resources is more likely to negatively impact business growth, and increase business risk, than climate change or natural disasters. However, as both climate change and natural disasters have the potential to create resource scarcity, they are related concerns. An additional worry is the political and social instability that could result from a dearth of natural resources; for example, a conflict over a lack of quality drinking water, or healthy land to grow food. As any kind of instability can substantially disrupt supply chain operations, the impact of climate change and natural disasters cannot be disregarded as a potential business threat.[1] In short, the same concerns that are encouraging human interest in sustainability have very practical applications for industry. Moreover, these concerns are all interrelated, as shown in Figure 6.1.

Different industries see these threats through different lenses. For example, resource scarcity and political instability are perceived as major risks to those in the automotive, metals, oil and gas, engineering and construction, and industrial manufacturing industries. On the other

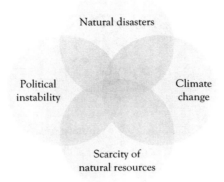

Figure 6.1. Supply chain threats.

hand, climate change and natural disaster are more significant to those in industries like insurance, utilities, transportation and logistics, banking, and consumer goods.[2] Clearly, companies that proactively attempt to reduce their exposure to these risks with a sustainable supply chain strategy will be in a better position to address these threats, if and when they surface, than reactive competitors who have no understanding of the issues, and are not prepared at all.

Thus, in this final chapter, we go beyond the basic issues and solutions presented in this book to explain what's on the horizon for sustainable supply chain management. Radical product and process innovation, sustainable purchasing, and product end-of-life activities are specifically discussed.

Radical Product and Process Innovation

Over the last decade, more companies have jumped on the sustainability bandwagon and worked to improve the energy and water efficiency of their products and supply chains. While these efforts have paid off, as indicated by the internal efficiency metrics of many companies (i.e., measurements of resources used per unit of product produced), many are also starting to recognize that these efficiency gains are plateauing, due to a heavy reliance on incremental improvements to existing products and processes to make changes, versus more substantial modes

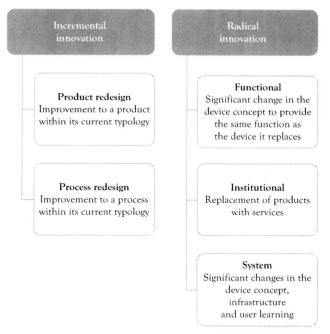

Figure 6.2. Incremental vs. radical innovation.

of improvement. In the future, "radical" innovations will be required to significantly reduce resource use—that is, to go beyond the low-hanging fruit. **Radical innovations** require new ways of doing things, unlike **incremental innovations**, which simply improve existing products and processes. Examples of incremental and radical innovations, their drivers, and their organizational impacts are provided in the following case, and illustrated in Figure 6.2.

Example: Electrolux Washing Machines and Eco-Innovation[3]

An example of a company that chose to tackle sustainability issues with radical innovation is the Electrolux Company, a European maker of household appliances. Washing machines in the EU consume as much electricity as the entire country of Portugal. This is, in part, because most European homes keep their machines until they can no longer be repaired; thus more than 40 million inefficient machines exist in the market today. Washing machines today use 60% less energy and 65% less water per kilogram of washing than do machines from the 1980s. However, between 2005 and 2007, the average efficiency of producers' machines improved by less than 2%, and the marginal improvements have continued to decrease, indicating an industry plateau.

An example of an incremental innovation that has occurred with Electrolux's machines is its use of energy rating improvement goals. Over the last decade, most washing machine manufacturers have moved their lines from an energy rating of "A" to an "A+," in response to consumer demand. An "A" rated machine uses 0.19 or fewer kilowatts of energy to wash a kilogram of clothing, while an "A+" frontloading machine uses 0.17 or fewer kilowatts per kilogram of clothing. Today, the majority of machines produced by Electrolux meet the "A+" rating, and the company is working to move its machines toward an "A++" rating, which would use less than 0.15 kilowatts of energy per kilogram of clothing washed. These gains have been achieved by using more efficient motors, increasing capacity, optimizing cycles, and minimizing the clearance between the inner and outer washing drum, reducing water use and the energy needed to heat water. Clearly, all of these innovations are improvements to existing processes or parts designs—that is, they are incremental innovations.

To break through the efficiency plateau, and to incentivize consumers to buy more efficient machines, Electrolux decided to also introduce several radical innovations.

The first example, the IronAid, is considered a **functionally radical innovation**. The IronAid is a condenser tumble dryer with a steam generating unit inside. The product can dry clothes like a typical tumble dryer, but its steam capabilities can also be used to remove wrinkles and odors from clothing, thus eliminating the need for washing, drying, and ironing. This capability was developed in direct response to constraints on consumers' washing abilities; interestingly, most wash loads consist of clothing that is not clean but also not dirty—it just requires freshening. Thus, considerable environmental benefits can be achieved by enabling consumers to bypass the unnecessary washing and drying that were once required to freshen clothes, should consumers want to do so.

The second example, an **institutionally radical innovation**, occurs when a service replaces a product purchase. At Electrolux, this is the Electrolux Product Service System, designed to reduce consumer retention of old, inefficient machines, and better enable product take-back. With this program, Electrolux installs a new, energy efficient machine in a customer's home and maintains ownership of the machine. The machine is connected to the home's smart meter to measure electricity usage per load. The customer pays a certain amount for machine installation and then a certain amount per wash load (measured by the smart meter). Electrolux monitors the machine online, and then replaces the machine after a certain number of cycles. The retired machine then goes back to the factory for refurbishment.

In the third and most advanced type of innovation, **system radical innovation**, significant changes are made to a device's basic concept and the systems that surround and support that concept, like infrastructure and user knowledge. At Electrolux, one radical system innovation concept is to create a washing machine that works with a house's "system" in a completely different way. If designed correctly, a washing machine could use heated water already used by other appliances or household systems, in lieu of sourcing new water for washing. In such a hypothetical new machine, illustrated in Figure 6.3, a user would place their clothing in the machine and select the material type, and the machine would weigh the clothing and dispense an appropriate amount of detergent. The machine would then evaluate other household appliances and energy sources to find

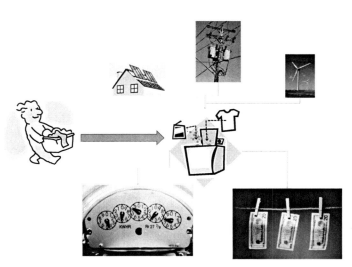

Figure 6.3. Washing machine system radical innovation.

thermal energy and reusable water (e.g., the dishwasher, the refrigerator, the dryer, household solar or wind systems), and connect back to the electricity grid for information on current demand and pricing. The machine could then calculate the cheapest and most efficient use of energy and water, and advise the user on the best time to start their washing, given the cost and environmental impact of the various options available.

Sustainable Purchasing

Just as with product and process design, trends are afoot in the sustainable purchasing field. Specifically, it appears that an increasing number of companies, government entities, and nonprofits are adopting sustainable purchasing policies. In suit, suppliers should expect to see sustainability criteria appearing more often in Requests for Proposals, thus making this an influential factor in supplier selection. Suppliers should also anticipate having to respond to sustainability questionnaires and scorecards with more frequency, and being asked to comply with codes of conduct, and reporting and auditing requirements, on a more regular basis.

Those that have already adopted sustainability policies, programs, and evaluation and reporting methods—like internal metrics and scorecards—are likely going to be asked to add to and modify their criteria, using additional and new ranking thresholds and benchmarks. Currently, the basic reporting categories touch on greenhouse gas emissions, waste, energy, and water management. However, social issues will increasingly be addressed, like diversity and inclusion efforts.

There are growth opportunities in the sustainability measurement and reporting industry, such as measurement and reporting software, and peer-based networks for sharing ideas about particular industries, like financial or health care services. Today, the purchasing targets that receive the most attention from professional services industries are office paper products, public statements and marketing materials, cleaning supplies and services, building materials, office furniture, office appliances and, not surprisingly, coffee.[4] Product producers will continue to emphasize measurement and reporting on significant inputs like water (particularly food and beverage producers), energy, and raw materials, along with waste outputs.

End-of-Life Activities: Reclaiming and Recycling Trends

Undoubtedly, a primary trend in product end-of-life management will be that the definition of toxic materials will continue to expand, as will bans on those materials. These bans will create opportunities for entrepreneurial activity, as we have already begun to see in Europe and parts of the United States. For example, some states ban landfill disposal of automotive shocks and struts due to their oil content. As a result, a major manufacturer of these products set up a program to collect the used shocks and struts and reclaim materials in them, particularly the specialized steel used in their manufacturing, which has a substantial market demand. In addition to the economic benefit, the company received positive marketing exposure for their environmental stance.

In the United States, recycling activity will continue to grow. The economic recession that commenced in 2008 caused prices for recycled paper, plastic, aluminum, and ferrous scrap metal to drop significantly; by the beginning of 2009, prices in some of these significant materials categories had seen a 22% to 31% decline. However, this price drop did not impact the amount of recycled material collected. By 2011, many of the prices for recycled products had returned to their pre-recession price levels, largely due to the high demand for these materials in China. There are some interesting phenomena for categories such as recovered paper, which faces significantly declining demand in domestic markets but increasing demand in the export market. With overall demand for recycled newspapers on the decline, this has led to paper recycler bankruptcies and closures. These trends are leading to consolidations by the bigger players, achieved through mergers and acquisitions.

Lacking a government industrial policy such as other countries have, the U.S. recycling market goes through swings in which used materials pile up, and are then depleted, with increasing amounts of recycling material exported to China. Other countries, like Japan, have put significant effort into processes that improve recycling and material separation, in addition to new material development. With the country facing a massive reconstruction effort, many materials are needed. However, recycling analysts project that China will eventually meet all its recycled material demand internally and that U.S. materials will become too costly to ship there. Thus, there is concern that without a U.S. industrial recycling strategy, the United States may lose a significant market for recycled materials and will not have manufacturing or products to replace the lost Chinese demand.[5]

Example: Recycling Christmas Lights in China[6]

Shijia, China, is the world capital for recycling of Christmas tree lights thrown away by Americans. Located about an hour from Guangzhou, Shijia has roughly ten factories that handle more than 20 million pounds of these lights annually. Several organizations and companies will take the old lights in the United States, but the vast majority of the lights are then bundled into bales and shipped to China for $.60/pound. Due to environmental issues and a lack of technology for processing the wires, virtually no U.S. scrap metal companies are willing to process it.

While China may not have curbside recycling like the United States, any waste product with a residual value in China is retrieved, sorted, and reused or reprocessed. Many would argue that China may in fact have more of a recycling culture than the United States because the waste is seen as a moneymaking opportunity rather than an environmentally motivated activity. Shijia is one of China's many recycling zones. Twenty years ago, the city became a recycling hub due to low environmental standards and cheap labor. Originally, the lighting wire was burned to remove the rubber or plastic coating and the valuable copper and brass recovered—a dirty, pollution-generating process. However, entrepreneurs and innovators eventually got involved and figured out a clean, water-based process to remove the coating from the metal so that the residual coating, glass, and metals could be resold. Today, the plastic and rubber insulating coating has found its way into a range of products, including slipper soles.

The United States, on the other hand, lacks industrial demand for these products. Without demand, the recycling industry does not have the incentive to invest in separation technology for wire, and must either landfill the insulation or sell it as a very low cost fuel to power plants. For recyclers, sending the wire to China makes the most economic sense. While some may ponder how offshoring recycling activities is sustainable, others may ask how sustainable it is for Americans to throw away millions of pounds of lighting each year because of one broken bulb in their strand.

Conclusion

The goal of this book was to educate managers, executives, entrepreneurs, and other stakeholders about sustainable supply chain management. In this final chapter, we presented the trends and opportunities that are emerging in the field. We hope to have adequately conveyed the strategic importance of adopting a sustainability focus in your company's supply chain, regardless of your industry or position. While different managers may not agree on the threat of climate change or the importance of social or environmental sustainability, all should agree that resource depletion and various sources of instability are very real threats to the economic performance of companies, as is the fact that other countries are ahead of the U.S. in their policies and their innovations. Proactive managers will find that incorporating sustainability ideas into their supply chain management will give them a leg up on their competitors.

Recommended Readings and Videos

- Electrolux (2011) TED Lecture About the Magic Washing Machine, June 10, 2011. Retrieved on December 29, 2011 from http://group.electrolux.com/en/ted-lecture-about-the-magic-washing-machine-9634/
- Video on the Christmas Light Recycling Plant can be accessed from http://www.theatlantic.com/international/archive/2011/12/the-chinese-town-that-turns-your-old-christmas-tree-lights-into-slippers/250190/

List of Acronyms

ADF	Advanced disposal fee
C2C	Cradle to Cradle
CFP	Corporate financial performance
CSP	Corporate social performance
DfD	Design for Disassembly
DfE	Design for the Environment
DIFOT	Delivery in full and on time
EEE	Electrical and electronic equipment
EMS	Environmental management system
EOL	Product end-of-life management
EPR	Extended product responsibility
GHG	Greenhouse gas
ISO	International Organization for Standardization
KPI	Key performance indicator
LCA	Life cycle assessment, or life cycle analysis
LCC	Life cycle cost
LCI	Life cycle Inventory
NGO	Nongovernmental organization
QFD	Quality Function Deployment
QFDE	Quality Function Deployment for the Environment
SSCM	Sustainable supply chain management
SWOT	Strengths, Weaknesses, Opportunities, Threats
TNS	The Natural Step
WEEE	Waste electrical and electronic equipment

Glossary

Advanced disposal fee: Fees imposed by waste management entities to subsidize the cost of properly processing or disposing of toxic or problematic materials, like solvents, oil, and tires

Biomimicry: A design approach in which data about the functioning of biological systems is used to help solve engineering problems

Business plan: A plan written to assist with the business launch process, typically describing a company's purpose and goals; the company's ownership structure; the company's service or product line; the market for those services or products; managerial, marketing, sales, and other essential launch strategies; and financial projections; often used to obtain seed funding

Certification: A mechanism used to verify claims made by a company; third party certification offers the most assurance that a company's claims are objectively true

Closed loop supply chain: A supply chain in which all outputs, including used products, are recaptured for use as inputs in new manufacturing or consumption processes

Code of conduct: A clear standard articulated by buyers for suppliers regarding labor practices and the manufacturing or production environment

Competitive advantage: Sustained, superior performance over competitors in the marketplace, achieved through a unique exploitation of external operating conditions, or a unique utilization of internal competencies and capabilities

Corporate philanthropy: A business practice in which some of a company's operating profits are directed to social and environmental causes, often through an associated foundation

Corporate social responsibility: A business practice in which a company seeks to follow socially and environmentally responsible business principles as it conducts its work

Cost leadership: A business strategy in which profitability is primarily derived and maintained by managing and minimizing costs

Cradle to Cradle: A design approach and certification program based on industrial ecology principles, developed by William McDonough and Michael Bruangart

Credence attribute: A product or process attribute that is difficult for a purchaser to perceive through observation

Design for Disassembly: An approach to designing new products that considers their future disassembly, recycling, and reuse possibilities

Design for the Environment: A design and analysis framework that considers the complete environmental and health impact of a product or process, from material extraction to disposal

Differentiation: A business strategy in which profitability is derived by promoting the real or perceived value of products sold to consumers

Ecoefficiency: An efficiency measure that focuses on resource inputs like processing steps, waste, and toxic product use, relative to the desired outputs of a process; "ecoefficiencies" are the actions and steps that companies take to promote improvement in ecoefficiency measures

Environmental management system: A set of processes and practices that can enable an organization to reduce its environmental impact and increase its operating efficiency

Extended product responsibility: A concept in which manufacturers or producers take responsibility for the final disposal of a product after its sale to and use by a consumer

First party claim: A claim in which the supplier or producer (the first party) states that they have produced their products a certain way

Forward supply chain: A linear and one-directional supply chain in which inputs are turned into outputs

Functionally radical innovation: An innovation in which there is a significant change in the design or functioning of a device concept

Incremental innovation: Innovations that improve existing products and processes

Industrial ecology: A framework that views business as a series of material and energy flows, in which the material and energy outputs of one process become the inputs for another

Input: A resource used in a production process (materials, plants, animals, human labor, etc.)

Institutionally radical innovation: An innovation in which a service replaces a product purchase

ISO 14000: A family of guidelines covering multiple aspects of environmental management systems, issued by the International Organization for Standards

ISO 26000: A family of guidelines covering seven aspects of social responsibility, issued by the International Organization for Standards

Key performance indicator: A measurement of performance, typically designed to monitor significant economic, environmental, and social activities

Life cycle assessment: Also known as life cycle analysis; a quantitative assessment of a product's sustainability impact, from raw materials sourcing through the end of a product's useful life

Life cycle cost: The total cost of owning, operating, maintaining, and disposing of a product

Output: The products of a production process (consumer goods, waste, information, etc.)

Product end-of-life management: The process of planning, implementing, and controlling the efficient, cost effective flow of raw materials, in-process inventory, and finished goods from the point of consumption back to the point of origin for the purpose of recapturing value or proper disposal

Quality Function Deployment for the Environment: A tool used to translate the functional and environmental needs of stakeholders into appropriate product design features

Radical innovation: Innovations that create completely new ways of doing things

Readily apparent attribute: A product attribute that is easily perceived by consumers through observation—e.g., color, size, and price

Recycling with disassembly: A recycling method in which used products are disassembled prior to recycling, which can assist with grouping of like materials for recycling, lessened contamination of recyclable materials, higher recovery rates, and improved reuse or resale

Recycling without disassembly: A recycling method in which used products cannot or are not disassembled prior to recycling, instead being prepared for recycling by being ground, shredded, shattered, or compressed; because products are not disassembled before processing, sorting of component materials can be difficult, contamination is common, and recovery rates can be low

Reverse supply chain: The structure, processes, and systems that allow materials and products to be brought back to a company for reuse or reprocessing

Second party claim: A claim in which a purchasing entity (second party) certifies that a producer (first party) has met a certain set of guidelines; can be collusive in nature

Social enterprise: An organization or business that seeks to create direct social or environmental benefit through its operations

Strategic plan: A long term plan that establishes an overall direction for a company as it strives to achieve competitive advantage; manifested by a company's day-to-day operations

Supplier management system: A set of processes and practices to help buyers consistently evaluate and move suppliers toward sustainability targets

Supplier scorecard: An internally generated tool that measures supplier activities in relation to an organization's strategy and mission

Supplier tier: A stage of a supply chain in which a certain task is done or in which a certain value is added to a product; for example, first tier suppliers often do final product assembly, and are closest in proximity in the supply chain structure to the company branding and selling the product being manufactured

System radical innovation: An innovation in which significant changes are made to a device's basic concept, as well as the systems that surround and support that concept, like infrastructure and user knowledge

Take-back: The act of bringing used consumer products back to the manufacturer or to a contracted entity for reuse, recycling, or proper disposal

The Natural Step: An analytical framework based on a set of irrefutable scientific principles from physics and natural law, stipulating four guiding conditions for becoming a sustainable society

Third party claim: A claim in which an independent party (third party) with no vested interest in an outcome certifies that a producer (first party) has met certain standards

Triple bottom line: The notion that social, environmental, and economic performance are all essential for business success; also known as "people, planet, and profit"

Value-added: A product that has undergone some form of processing that adds additional worth or value to the original entity or raw material

Value chain: The activities in which a business engages that add value to products or services for consumers; not all businesses do all of the activities required to create value added products or services

Value stream mapping: A type of analysis in which designers reconstruct a particular process on paper to determine if each step in the process is adding value to the entity under review, or simply generating waste

Notes

Chapter 1

1. World Commission on Environment and Development (1987).
2. Jackson (ND).
3. IBS Center for Management Research (2002).
4. Apple, Inc. (2007b), pp. 1–4.
5. Apple, Inc. (2011), pp. 18–25.
6. Apple, Inc. (2011), pp. 16.
7. Apple, Inc. (ND).
8. Levi Strauss & Company (2010).
9. Nike, Inc. (2009).
10. Kristof (2009), p. A35.
11. United Nations Global Compact.
12. The Kroger Co. (2011).
13. Environmental Leader (2007); CNN Money (2011).
14. Gunther (2006).
15. Plambeck and Denend (2008), pp. 55–57.
16. Apple, Inc. (2007a).
17. Author's notes.
18. Margolis, Elfenbein, and Walsh (2007), p. 22.
19. Margolis, Elfenbein, and Walsh (2007), p. 26.
20. Author's notes.
21. Lacy, et al. (2010), p. 11.
22. Little (2004).
23. Casey (2007).
24. Lacy, et al., p. 20.
25. MIT Sloan Management Review and the Boston Consulting Group (2011), p. 9.
26. MIT Sloan Management Review and the Boston Consulting Group (2011), p. 9.
27. Lacy, et al., p. 14.

Chapter 2

1. Mycoskie (2011), pp. 69–70.
2. Little (2004).

3. Patagonia (2011b).
4. Little (2004).
5. Patagonia (2011a).
6. Barney (2001).
7. Centinkaya et al. (2011).
8. Centinkaya et al. (2011).
9. Reproduced from author notes, with the permission of Sattie Clark of Eleek.
10. Reproduced from author notes, with the permission of Sattie Clark of Eleek.
11. Marshall et al. (2009).
12. U.S. Department of Commerce (2009).
13. U.S. Department of Commerce (2009).
14. Green Toys, Inc. (2010).
15. Centinkaya et al. (2011).

Chapter 3

1. Manget et al. (2009).
2. Food Product Design (2011).
3. Larson, A. (2009).
4. York, J. (2006).
5. Masui et al. (2003), pp. 90–106.
6. Pullman, Moore, and Wardell (2002), pp. 354–364.
7. Garcilaso (2004).
8. Natural Step (2011).
9. Dilley, M. (2010).
10. McDonough and Braungart (2002).
11. McDonough and Braungart (2011).
12. Lee and Bony (2009).
13. Herman Miller (2010).
14. Benyus, J. (1997).
15. Ask Nature (2011).
16. InterFace (2012).

Chapter 4

1. China Digital Times (2011).
2. Environmental Leader (2010).
3. Brammer et al. (2011).

4. Duhigg and Barboza (2012), p. A1.
5. Peterson (1996), pp. 28–31.
6. ISO (2004).
7. ISO (2011).
8. *The Economist* (2011), pp. 14–18.
9. *The Economist* (2011), pp. 14–18.
10. Brammer et al. (2011).
11. Sroufe (2006), pp. 3–23.
12. Food Alliance (2011).
13. Procter & Gamble (2009).
14. PR Newswire (2011).
15. Kam et al. (2006), pp. 103–115.

Chapter 5

1. Rogers and Tibben-Lembke (1998).
2. Rogers and Tibben-Lembke (1998).
3. Rogers and Tibben-Lembke (1998).
4. Brief Introduction of Directive 2002/96/EC on Waste Electrical and Electronic Equipment (2003).
5. Pagell, Wu, and Murthy (2007), pp. 133–143.
6. Geyer and Jackson (2004), pp. 55–73.
7. U.S. Life Cycle Inventory Database (2010).
8. Woolridge, Ward, Phillips, Collins, and Gandy (2006, January), pp. 94–103.
9. Patagonia: Common Threads Initiative (2011).
10. Pagell, Wu, and Murthy (2007), pp. 133–143.
11. Fabrycky (1987).
12. Ulrich and Pearson (1998), pp. 352–369.
13. Ulrich and Pearson (1998), pp. 352–369.
14. Lee and Bony (2009).
15. Staples (2011).
16. Kodak Single Use Camera Recycling (2011).
17. Geyer and Jackson (2004), pp. 55–73.
18. Geyer and Jackson (2004), pp. 55–73.
19. Pagell, Wu, and Murthy (2007), pp. 133–143.
20. U.S. Environmental Protection Agency (2009).
21. Rogers (2011), pp. 10–17.
22. White (2004).
23. Fluensee (2011).

24. Nielson (2008).
25. American Beverage Association (2010).
26. Barelline (2008).
27. Dell (2011).

Chapter 6

1. PWC (2011).
2. PWC (2011).
3. Smith (2008).
4. Strandberg (2010).
5. Powell (2011).
6. Minter (2011).

References

American Beverage Association (2010). Packaging. *Environment.* Retrieved December 19, 2011, from http://www.ameribev.org/environment/packaging/

Apple, Inc. (2007a). *A greener Apple.* Retrieved September 4, 2011, from Apple, Inc: http://www.apple.com/hotnews/agreenerapple/

Apple, Inc. (2007b). *Final assembly supplier audit report,* pp. 1–4.

Apple, Inc. (2011). *Apple supplier responsibility progress report,* pp. 18–25.

Apple, Inc. (ND). *Supplier responsibility: Beyond compliance.* Retrieved September 6, 2011, from Apple, Inc.: http://www.apple.com/supplierresponsibility/beyond-compliance.html

Ask Nature (2011). Lotusan® paint. Retrieved August 11, 2011 from http://www.asknature.org/product/6b8342fc3e784201e4950dbd80510455

Barelline, J. (2008). *HP reduces laptop packaging 97 percent for Wal-Mart.* Greenbix.com. Retrieved December 20, 2011, from http://www.greenbiz.com/news/2008/09/02/hp-reduces-laptop-packaging-97-percent-wal-mart.

Barney, J. B. (2001). *Gaining and sustaining competitive advantage* (2nd ed.). Upper Saddle River, NJ: Prentice Hall.

Benyus, J. (1997). *Biomimicry: Innovation inspired by nature.* New York: William Morrow and Company, Inc.

Brammer et al. (2011). *Managing sustainable global supply chains: A systematic review of the body of knowledge.* Network for Business Sustainability, Ivey Business School, University of Western Ontario, London, Ontario, Canada.

Brief Introduction of Directive 2002/96/EC on Waste Electrical and Electronic Equipment (2003). Retrieved December 8, 2011, from http://www.weeeregistration.com/weee-directive.html

Casey, S. (2007). Blueprint for green business. Retrieved January 7, 2012, from CNN Money: http://money.cnn.com/magazines/fortune/fortune_archive/2007/04/02/8403423/index.htm

Centinkaya, B., Cuthbertson, R., Ewer, G., Klaas-Wissing, T., Piotrowicz, W., & Tyssen, C. (2011). *Sustainable supply chain management: Practical ideas for moving toward best practice* (1st ed.). Heidelberg, Germany: Springer-Verlag.

China Digital Times (2011). *China reclaims former perch as world's biggest manufacturer.* Retrieved December 20, 2011 from http://chinadigitaltimes.net/2011/03/china-reclaims-former-perch-as-world%E2%80%99s-biggest-manufacturer/

Dell, (2011). *The three Cs: Innovations in computer packaging design.* Retrieved December 20, 2011, from http://content.dell.com/us/en/corp/d/corp-comm/earth-products-packaging

Dilley, M. (2010). *Max Hamburger and the natural step.* Creative Commons, The Natural Step. Retrieved August 9, 2011 from http://thenaturalstep.org/sites/all/files/Max-TNS-CaseStudy-FINAL.pdf

Duhigg, C., Barboza, D., (2012). In China, the human costs that are built into an iPad. *New York Times*, pp. A1.

Economist (2011). Following the footprints. *The Economist Technology Quarterly*, pp. 14–18.

Environmental Leader (2007). *Kroger opens energy-efficient store in Ohio.* Retrieved September 3, 2011, from Environmental Leader: http://www.environmentalleader.com/2007/03/05/kroger-opens-energy-efficient-store-in-ohio/ and CNN Money (2011). How green energy saves the Fortune 500 billions. Retrieved September 3, 2011, from CNNMoney: http://money.cnn.com/galleries/2011/fortune/1105/gallery.millions_green_energy_savings.fortune/5.html

Environmental Leader (2010). *Wal-Mart Pledges to Cut Supply Chain Emissions 20M Metric Tons by 2015.* Environmental Leader, February 26, 2010. Retrieved December 20, 2011 from http://www.environmentalleader.com/2010/02/26/walmart-pledges-to-cut-supply-chain-emissions-20m-metric-tons-by-2015/

Fabrycky, W. (1987). Designing for life cycle. *Mechanical Engineering*, January.

Fluensee (2011). *RFID Keg tracking: New Belgium Brewery case study.* Retrieved January 6, 2011, from http://www.fluensee.com/downloads/Case_Study_NBB_Keg_Tracking.pdf

Food Alliance (2011). How Decisions are Made. Retrieved July 11, 2011, from http://foodalliance.org/certification/how-it-works

Food Product Design (2011). *75% of European shoppers prefer sustainable products.* Retrieved August 4, 2011 from http://www.foodproductdesign.com/news/2011/03/75-of-european-shoppers-prefer-sustainable-produc.aspx

Garcilaso, L. (2004). *Life cycle analysis of paper and plastic bags*, Michigan Environmental Education Curriculum. Retrieved August 20, 2011 from http://techalive.mtu.edu/meec/module14/title.htm

Geyer, R., & Jackson, T. (2004). Supply loops and their constraints: The industrial ecology of recycling and reuse. *California Management Review 46*(2), 55–73.

Green Toys, Inc. (2010,). Green Toys Inc. goes global. Retrieved January 11, 2012, from http://www.greentoys.com/PressReleases/GT-Europe-Distribution-ReleaseFINAL.htm

Gunther, M. (2006). *Organic for everyone, the Wal-Mat Way.* Retrieved September 4, 2011, from CNNMoney: http://money.cnn.com/2006/07/25/news/companies/pluggedin_gunther_cotton.fortune/

Herman M. (2010). *Building a Better World Annual Report.* Retrieved August 11, 20011 from http://www.hermanmiller.com/MarketFacingTech/hmc/about_us/Environmental_Advocacy/2010_A_Better_World_Report.pdf

IBS Center for Management Research (2002). *Nike's labor practices, ICMR case BECG018.* Retrieved June 23, 2011, from http://www.icmrindia.org/casestudies/catalogue/Business%20Ethics/Nike%20Labor%20Practices.htm

InterFace (2012). Interface FLOR, Retrieved January 6, 2012 from http://www.interfaceflor.com/default.aspx?Section=2&Sub=3

ISO (2004). ISO 14000 Essentials. Retrieved July 7, 2011, from http://www.iso.org/iso/iso_14000_essentials

ISO (2011). Discovering ISO 26000. Retrieved July 7, 2011, from http://www.iso.org/iso/iso_catalogue/management_and_leadership_standards/social_responsibility/sr_discovering_iso26000.htm

Jackson, R. (ND). *Managing human rights risk in the supply chain.* Retrieved August 18, 2011, from simoncroom.com, sourced from STR Responsible Sourcing: http://www.supply-chain.org.uk/documents/STR-RSManagingHumanRightsRiskinSupplyChains.pdf

Kam et al. (2006). Strategic business operations, freight transport and eco-efficiency: A conceptual model. In J. Sarkis (Ed.), *Greening the supply chain* (pp.103–115). Worcester, MA: Springer.

Kodak Single Use Camera Recycling (2011). Retrieved December 10, 2011, from http://www.kodak.com/ek/US/en/Global_Sustainability/Health_Safety_and_Environment/HSE_Support_Center/Product_End_of_Life_Management/Single_Use_Cameras.htm

Kristof, K. (2009) Where sweatshops are a dream. *New York Times,* pp. A35.

Kroger Co., The (2011). *Sustainability Report,* pp. 15.

Lacy, P., Cooper, T., Hayward, R., Neuberger, L. (2010). *A new era of sustainability.* Accenture and the United Nations Global Compact, pp. 11.

Larson, A. (2009). *Sustainability and innovation: Frameworks, concepts, and tools for product and strategy redesign.* University of Virginia Darden Business Publishing, Charlottesville, VA. UV 4272.

Lee, D., & L. Bony (2009). *Cradle to cradle design at Herman Miller: Moving toward environmental sustainability.* Harvard Business School, Cambridge: MA. HBS 9-607-003.

Levi Strauss & Company (2010). *Frequently asked questions about LS & Co. Global sourcing practices,* pp. 6. Retrieved August 19, 2011, from Levi Strauss & Co: Sustainability: Product: Product Suppliers: At the Factory: http://www.levistrauss.com/sites/default/files/librarydocument/2010/4/global-sourcing-practices-faqs-20100513.pdf

Little, A. G. (2004). Patagonia founder on politics, saving Earth. *Grist magazine.* Retrieved September 6, 2011, from MSNBC.com: http://www.msnbc.

msn.com/id/6353516/ns/us_news-environment/t/patagonia-clothing-founder-ponders-politics-saving-earth/

Manget et al. (2009). *Capturing the green advantage for consumer companies*, Boston Consulting Group: Boston, January 2009.

Margolis, J., Elfenbein, H. A., Walsh, J. P. (2007). *Does it pay to be good? A meta-analysis and redirection of research on the relationship between corporate social and financial performance.* Seminar Paper retrieved from Harvard Business School, pp. 22.

Marshall, S., Pullman, M., Anderson, Z., Flax, M., Gambetta, D., Green-Powell, J., (2009). *Sustainability Amidst uncertainty: Columbia forest products' pursuit of sustainability in a changing market.* Center for Global Leadership in Sustainability Case, Portland, OR: Portland State University.

Masui et al. (2003). *Applying quality function deployment to environmentally conscious design. International Journal of Quality and Reliability Management 20*(1), 90–106.

McDonough, W., & Braungart, M. (2002). *Cradle to cradle: Remaking the way we make things.* New York: Northpoint Press.

McDonough, W., & Braungart, M. (2011). *Cradle to cradle framework.* Retrieved August 9, 20011 from http://www.mbdc.com/detail.aspx?linkid=1&sublink=6

Minter, A. (2011). *The Chinese Town That Turns Your Old Christmas Tree Lights into Slippers. The Atlantic,* December, 2011. Retrieved December 30, 2011 from http://www.theatlantic.com/international/archive/2011/12/the-chinese-town-that-turns-your-old-christmas-tree-lights-into-slippers/250190/

MIT Sloan Management Review and the Boston Consulting Group (2011). *Research Report: Sustainability: the 'Embracers' Seize Advantage* (Winter), pp. 9.

Mycoskie, B. (2011). *Start something that matters.* New York: Spiegel & Grau, pp. 69–70.

Natural Step (2011). *The four systems conditions.* Retrieved August 9, 2011 from http://thenaturalstep.org/the-system-conditions

Nielson (2008). *Packaging and the environment: A global Nielson consumer report.* Retrieved December 20, 2011, from http://pl.nielsen.com/trends/documents/NielsenGlobalPackagingEnviroReportMar08.pdf

NIKE, Inc. (2009). *Corporate responsibility report.* Retrieved August 19, 2011, from Nike, Inc.: Workers & Factories: Key Issues: http://www.nikebiz.com/crreport/content/workers-and-factories/3-1-4-our-strategy-evolving-approach.php?cat=overview

Pagell, M., Wu, Z., & N. Murthy (2007). The supply chain implications of recycling. *Business Horizons 50,* 133–143.

Patagonia (2011a). *Company info: Corporate responsibility, frequently asked questions.* Retrieved December 22, 2011, from http://www.patagonia.com/us/patagonia.go?assetid=37493

Patagonia (2011b). *The footprint chronicles: Digging deeper.* Retrieved December 22, 2011, from http://www.patagonia.com/us/footprint/index.jsp

Patagonia: Common Threads Initiative (2011). Retrieved December 6, 2011, from http://www.patagonia.com/us/common-threads?sssdmh=dm23.14269 8&src=112811_mt1

Peterson, J. (1996). Stop it or shrink it. *Purchasing Today* (July, 1996), pp. 28–31.

Plambeck, E. L., Denend, L. (2008). Case study: The greening of Wal-Mart. *Stanford Social Innovation Review*, 55–57.

Powell, J. (2011). Recycling 2011: Important Recycling Market Trend. *Resource recycling*, Portland, OR. Retrieved December 22, 2011 from http://www.cra 2011.org/presentations/Jerry%20Powell%20Markets.pdf.

PR Newswire (2011). P&G First Year Supplier Sustainability Scorecard Results in Collaboration and Innovation. April 7, 2011. Retrieved on July 12, 2011, from http://www.prnewswire.com/news-releases/pg-first-year-supplier-sustainability-scorecard-results-in-collaboration-and-innovation-119405714.html

Procter & Gamble (2009). *Supplier environmental sustainability scorecard and training materials.* Retrieved July 12, 2011, from http://www.pgsupplier.com/ supplier-environmental-sustainability-scorecard

Pullman, M., Moore, W., & Wardell, D. (2002). *A comparison of quality function deployment and conjoint analysis in new product design. Journal of Product Innovation Management 19*(5), 354–364.

PWC (2011). *CEOs on sustainable growth: Five areas of focus through 2014.* Retrieved December 26, 2011 from http://www.pwc.com/us/en/corporate-sustainability-climate-change/publications/sustainable-growth-us-ceo-survey.jhtml

Rogers, D. (2011). Sustainability is free-the case for doing the right thing. *Supply Chain Management Review*, pp. 10–17.

Rogers, D., & Tibben-Lembke (1998). Going backwards: Reverse logistics trends and practices. *Reverse Logistics Executive Council.*

Smith, B. (2008). *Toward Radical Eco-Innovation: Fabric Care at Electrolux*, IIIEE Master of Science Thesis, Lund, Sweden, October 2008.

Sroufe, R. (2006). A framework for strategic environmental sourcing. In J. Sarkis (Ed.), *Greening the supply chain* (pp. 3–23). Worcester, MA: Springer.

Staples (2011). Retrieved December 10, 2011, from http://www.staples.com/ sbd/cre/products/3dollar_inkrecycle/index.html

Strandberg, C. (2010). *Global scan of sustainable purchasing practices*, Strandberg Consulting, September, 2010. Retrieved December 22, 2011 from http:// www.buysmartbc.com/_Library/Resources/BSN_Summary_of_Practices_ Insurance_2011.pdf

Ulrich, K., & Pearson, S. (1998). Assessing the importance of design through product archaeology. *Management Science 44*(3), 352–369.

United Nations Global Compact. *Human rights and business dilemmas forum: Child labour*. Retrieved August 22, 2011, from http://human-rights. unglobalcompact.org/dilemmas/child-labour/

U.S. Department of Commerce (2009). *Industry report: Dolls, toys, games, and children's vehicles*; NAICS Code 33993. Retrieved January 11, 2012, from http://ita.doc.gov/td/ocg/toyoutlook_09.pdf

U.S. Environmental Protection Agency. (2009). *Municipal solid waste generation, recycling, and disposal in the United States detailed tables and figures for 2008*. Office of Resource Conservation and Recovery. Retrieved December 19, 2011, from http://www.epa.gov/epawaste/nonhaz/municipal/pubs/msw2008data.pdf

U.S. Life Cycle Inventory Database (2010). Retrieved December 8, 2011, from http://www.nrel.gov/lci/assessments.html

White, M. (2004). *Overview of the US pallet industry presentation*. Retrieved December 19, 2011, from http://unitload.vt.edu/presentations/Korea.pdf

Woolridge, A., Ward, G., Phillips, P., Collins, M., & Gandy, S. Life cycle assessment for reuse/recycling of donated waste textiles compared to use of virgin material: An UK energy saving perspective. *Resources, Conservation and Recycling 46*(1), 94–103.

World Commission on Environment and Development (1987). *Our common future (The Tokyo Declaration)*, pp. 8. Retrieved September 6, 2011, from Regjeringen.no: http://www.regjeringen.no/upload/SMK/Vedlegg/Taler%20 og%20artikler%20av%20tidligere%20statsministre/Gro%20Harlem%20 Brundtland/1987/Address_at_Eighth_WCED_Meeting.pdf

York, J. (2006). *Nike: Moving down the sustainability track through chemical substitution and waste reduction*. University of Virginia Darden Business Publishing, Charlottesville, VA. UV 0814.

Index

Announcing the Business Expert Press Digital Library

Concise E-books Business Students Need for Classroom and Research

This book can also be purchased in an e-book collection by your library as

- a one-time purchase,
- that is owned forever,
- allows for simultaneous readers,
- has no restrictions on printing, and
- can be downloaded as PDFs from within the library community.

Our digital library collections are a great solution to beat the rising cost of textbooks. e-books can be loaded into their course management systems or onto student's e-book readers.

The **Business Expert Press** digital libraries are very affordable, with no obligation to buy in future years. For more information, please visit **www.businessexpertpress.com/librarians**. To set up a trial in the United States, please contact **Adam Chesler** at *adam.chesler@businessexpertpress. com* for all other regions, contact **Nicole Lee** at *nicole.lee@igroupnet.com.*

OTHER TITLES IN OUR SUPPLY AND OPERATIONS MANAGEMENT COLLECTION

Collection Editor: **M. Johnny Rungtusanatham, The Ohio State Univerisity**

- *Design, Analysis and Optimization of Supply Chains: A System Dynamics Approach* by William Killingsworth
- *Supply Chain Planning and Analytics: The Right Product in the Right Place at the Right Time* by Gerald Feigin
- *Supply-Chain Survival in the Age of Globalization* by James A. Pope
- *Better Business Decisions Using Cost Modeling For Procurement, Operations, and Supply Chain Professionals* by Victor Sower and Christopher Sower
- *Supply Chain Risk Management Tools for Analysis* by David Olson
- *Leading and Managing the Lean Management Process* by Gene Fliedner
- *Supply Chain Information Technology* by David Olson
- *Global Supply Chain Management* by Matt Drake
- *Managing Commodity Price Risk: A Supply Chain Perspective* by George A. Zsidisin and Janet Hartley
- *RFID for the Supply Chain and Operations Professional* by Pamela Zelbst and Victor Sower